POACHERS AND POISONED OWLS

Poachers & Poisoned Owls

Tales of a Country Policeman's Wife

Romy Wyeth

EX LIBRIS PRESS

Published in 1997 by
EX LIBRIS PRESS
1 The Shambles
Bradford on Avon
Wiltshire
BA15 1JS

Design and typesetting by Ex Libris Press

Covers printed by Shires Press
Trowbridge, Wiltshire

Printed and bound by Cromwell Press
Broughton Gifford, Wiltshire

ISBN 0 948578 87 4

Contents

Wedlock in Wellingtons

From the moment I married a country copper life has never been predictable. In our years in a rural police station in Wiltshire we have had unexploded shells in the rosebed, stolen cars on the lawn and once a bag of human remains, thankfully prehistoric, in the office.

Suddenly I found myself the untrained half of a partnership in community policing, making it up as I went along, adjusting not just to life under a microscope but having to make the transition from townie to country ways while the locals watched to see how we would fit in.

My rural experience was limited, my few encounters with chickens had never succeeded in convincing me that they were not intent on pecking my ankles and, as my husband John never tires of reminding me, I must be one of the few people ever to be chased from a London park by an inquisitive pigeon.

I once indignantly heard Wyford Police Station described as a rather ugly red brick house. It has an office attached and stands in a quarter of an acre of garden which at the time we moved in had largely reverted to scrub.

From the back windows the view is straight from a picture

book – a farmyard and an ancient grey stone church nestling into a wooded hillside. The field behind houses, in the season, pheasant rearing pens, young heifers newly out to grass and sturdy rams prior to being put with the ewes. Throughout the winter months horses kick their heels, resplendent in waterproof blankets. In the spring the lambing pens are at the base of the Down, and as far as the eye can see the ewes graze with lambs at heel.

By spring my new husband had what was to be the first of many brainwaves: we would invest in some chickens to help clear the ground. So, with trepidation on my part and enthusiasm on John's, we took our first faltering steps into backyarding, with me keeping well away from those wicked beaks and beady eyes.

Mrs. F. was a white bantam cockerel named after my mother when we were still under the impression he was a hen. It took us a while to realise the strange noises Mrs. F. produced was the crow of a cockbird, but by then he was part of the family, so he stayed.

From the beginning he was a wanderer, flying over fences with ease to scratch at the newly planted vegetable plots. What was needed was a wing-clipping session, a skill we had yet to acquire but at which George Russell, our mentor in all things rural, was proficient. George is a real countryman, a well known character who was one third of the policing partnership in the area which encompassed some fifteen villages and hamlets. There were two rural police stations; George's home, Wazanik, had been the third – he bought it when it became redundant so still lived on his beat.

When his patrol brought him to Wyford, George decided to instruct John in this necessary art. We later learned that the evening when the birds are roosting is a far more suitable time for such endeavours. In the middle of the afternoon Mrs. F. had other plans.

He was wandering the lawn when George arrived. Round and

round the house he ran, followed by John brandishing the scissors, George in his uniform and me with a broom. Down the path, across the road with wings outstretched, complaining loudly, our frantic cockerel disappeared down the lane opposite and into the wild yonder. I admit to the mild hope that he was gone for good, but that night he returned to his harem and our hospitality.

Then one of the PC's who lived in the town decided he wanted a cockerel for stud ... at the time the idea seemed perfectly feasible, a way to brighten up the lives of his urban hens and encourage them to become broody.

One Sunday morning John set off for work with Mrs. F. in a sack in the back of the van. All went awry when they attempted to transfer the cockerel to his temporary home. As soon as the sack was opened the indignant bird took off into the local playing field and, despite the efforts of two police officers to trace the feathered fugitive while disclaiming all responsibility for him, no one had seen the agitated cockerel that morning.

My lunch time was brightened with the news that Mrs. F. had gone missing yet again, this time in the metropolis where he had no way of returning to the place he was meant to be. However, far from ending up in a cooking pot, he was found in the twilight, roosting in a hedge and taken to the police house he had been intended for. His stay was brief; the neighbours, unused to country sounds, did not appreciate a cock crowing in the early hours and he was returned to us forthwith.

🐓

I was totally unprepared for the next stage of organizing the garden – George Russell and his goats! The Russells are famous for their self-sufficiency: in 1974 they had several pregnant nannies and we were offered one of the kids. George decided that our need was greater than our confidence and set to work to convince John.

Jill Russell, a very practical lady, sent us some goat's milk to try, pointing out that to buy a nanny if we didn't like the milk was self-defeating. It took a while for me to summon up the courage to drink it, so sure was I that the taste would be horrid. Since those far-off days I have seen other people with that same suspicion in their eyes, politely take a sip and discover to their amazement that it is delicious. Goats' milk is creamier than cows', less is needed in hot drinks and, unless people are told, they are unaware of the difference. It has more body than bottled milk which now tastes insipid to my palate, and goat's milk has the added advantage that it can be frozen successfully.

First introductions to goats' milk will often come when on holiday in warmer climes. The heat, plus the fact that it is easily tainted by what the animal has eaten, has given the milk its undeservedly bad press. The secret is in the swift straining of the liquid through a sieve with either muslin or, more conveniently, a Man Size Kleenex tissue, while it is still warm, then its immediate placing in a fridge to cool. It does need to be drunk very cold for the best taste.

However, if we had a kid it would be two years before I had to get used to either drinking the milk or, horror of horrors, squatting by a goat's back legs and touching its udder. Little did I know!

We visited the Russells and for the first time were intro-

duced to those endearing, impossible and addictive animals that have since become part of our lives. At first glance they looked huge – their strange, slit pupils, almond-shaped but decidedly sinister eyes and their determined investigation of our hair, clothes and shoelaces with their mouths were distinctly unsettling.

Jill gave us a crash course in basic goat-keeping. John set to work building a goat shed out of old doors, with a tin roof and a dirt floor on which we piled a thick layer of soft straw to begin our deep-litter bedding. All we needed was our baby goat.

At last the day arrived – the goat produced two billies and a nanny. We were enchanted with the tiny creature with her pink muzzle and endless legs. Our first disappointment was that the nanny kid turned out to be an hermaphrodite, useless for anything except meat. This is something that goatkeepers are on the alert for when kids are born – an hermaphrodite possesses the reproductive parts of both sexes, neither of which are functional. A sign to note on an apparently female kid is a pea-shaped growth on the vulva or an enlarged clitoris. This can be difficult to certify for the novice goatkeeper but no animal should be passed on if there is any doubt.

In the case of billy kids only a few of the best bred are used for stud, the rest should either be put down at birth or raised to three or four months for meat. This has the flavour of young lamb and the market has been growing throughout the eighties and nineties for kid meat as palates become more adventurous.

All our hopes now centred on Sherry, a fifteen year-old black and white British Alpine who gave birth to one perfect white-faced kid who was to become our Snoopy. Now came the bombshell... the Russells had all the milk they needed and Jill suggested that instead of waiting for Snoopy to be weaned I learn to milk at once, so that Sherry might spend the summer with us.

I had in my moments of planning ahead come up with a formula for future milking. I would wear rubber gloves so that I wouldn't have to touch the dreaded udder, for some obscure reason a prospect my townie soul rejected. But Jill was a formidable lady and there was no way I dared turn up for my milking lessons in rubber gloves. I feared her scorn so fought to overcome my squeamishness.

Milking is a knack. Holding on to the teat near the bag and attempting to get the milk out is at first a hit-and-miss affair. Then suddenly it works and the milk begins to flow, but with wrist-aching slowness. The trick is not to pull but to open and shut the hands alternately, right at the top of the teat, a regular strong squeeze; with practice the milk flows easily. It is best to feed the nanny her concentrates at this time to keep her occupied. She then associates milking with food and behaves well.

Sherry was an eccentric character even by goat standards; she was a bony creature with a long and droopy udder. When she had had enough of my fumbling efforts to extract milk she played her strongest card and squatted. The udder would completely disappear into the bucket, her stomach would seal the top and there was no way I could get near the teats.

She loved Polo mints and hated her worming medicine: our first attempts at this necessary part of goat management were completely demoralising. Sherry was an old hand and she knew what the bottle signified. First she would cower at the end of her tether, then, as John grasped her collar and opened her mouth to put the bottle in, the air would be rent with her piteous cries. After a struggle, which usually resulted in half the medication going down his jeans, he would eventually manage to pour the potion down her protesting throat. Whereupon Sherry would lick her lips, shrug and get on with the important business of grazing. She knew who was in control and it was never possible to get the better of her.

Snoopy proved to be the biggest time waster and the best pet we could have chosen. Tiny and fearless, she followed me around the garden, into the uncarpeted hallway, racing up the stairs and back down three at a time, cavorting with high spirits at the bottom. She examined everything, her tiny nose quivering with interest, mouthing all the new things in her world. She practiced butting by pushing against any convenient part of my anatomy – her legs braced for maximum force – then fell asleep on my lap in the afternoon sun.

As she grew older she would take her titbits daintily, jumping and placing her hooves on our thighs, a habit she retained long into her adolescence, almost flattening us in the process. For the most part John managed to stand firm as a growing goatling, now as tall as he when on her hind legs, leapt boisterously at him. She loved to use my back as a platform when I was stooping to milk, a favourite trick of all goat kids. They wait until attention is diverted, then pounce on the unprotected and unsuspecting back.

Snoopy was happy to play with me all day but, if left alone without sight of her mother, she kicked up a determined fuss. I dreaded the inevitable day when Sherry returned to her rightful owners. I had realized that goats are herd animals – they adore company and unless I wanted to move into the goat shed we needed another animal.

❦

Again, as so often in the early years, it was the Russells to the rescue: they had a neighbour with a goat that needed a good home. We were uncertain that we would be suitable with our back garden run and occasional grazing as this animal had the run of an orchard. However, we passed muster and Holly came to stay.

There was to be a straight swop, Sherry going home and Holly coming to us on the return journey. I stayed at home with Snoopy expecting much ado when the pair were separated. In fact, for the first time ever, there was no outcry when Sherry was led off. The problems came later in the evening.

Holly was a brown and white Toggenburg; she looked like a walking hearthrug with floppy ears and a hoarse voice inherited from cross breeding in the past with a Nubian ancestor. In later years she became more moth-eaten to look at and we discovered she was allowing birds to perch on her back, pull out the long

coarse hair to line their nests. Birds were the only creatures ever to get above her in pecking order.

For the first time we witnessed the ritual greeting of two strange goats. Snoopy was by now nine months-old; she was sturdy and friendly, eager to please. Of indeterminate age, Holly was wary and prepared to do battle.

She reared high on her back legs, pranced briefly with her head on one side, came down on all fours and butted hard. Many times since that day I have observed the way strange goats size up each other. Frequently the butting is token only, but in the case of Snoopy and Holly very aggressive display, and very one-sided as the kid was unable to protect herself.

Worse was to come: John was out and as I checked the run on a cold frosty evening I found Snoopy huddled outside while Holly was in possession of the one-roomed stable. There was no way Holly intended to share. I was horrified – my precious baby goat was being bullied. Had we made a terrible mistake?

On John's return Holly was banished overnight to the garage and later the large chicken shed next door was pressed into temporary use as overspill quarters while he constructed a second stall. This done, peace reigned, the animals settling down once Holly had established who was boss.

Snoopy was used to being handled but I made a mistake when I allowed some local youngsters to play with her unsupervised. They began to tease her, shutting the stable door in her face. When I saw what was happening I sent the children home, but the damage was done. A few weeks later a friend brought her little girl to see the goats. Joanne toddled up to Snoopy who was tethered in the garden. Before anyone could move Snoopy's head went down and she charged, hitting the child in the midrift, knocking her over. Fortunately the little girl was more astonished than hurt but for the rest of Snoopy's life her mistrust of small people continued. Local children who came to see the livestock were warned always to keep the length of her chain away and never to go near her if she was loose.

❦

Meanwhile I was learning that there are no guidelines to being a police wife in a country station. Almost from the moment I arrived I became a cross between a secretary, an agony aunt and a speaking directory. There was nothing I wasn't expected to cope with, from where to take a poisoned owl to how to deal with an obscene phone call.

I learned to fill in the standard forms for lost and found property and unoccupied premises, to hand out shotgun and firearms applications and to be a sympathetic ear whenever necessary. Fortunately I had been a receptionist prior to our wedding so was used to dealing with the public, realising that however trivial the complaint being made the person making it had brought it to the police to sort out. If they got the untrained half of the partnership they still needed to air their grievance and be reassured. I took messages and passed them on, gradually becoming accustomed to my new role.

There were times when John was away and something happened that needed an urgent response. I hadn't been at Wyford long when one hot summer's day a neighbour brought a tall, thin and very bewildered old man to the door. He had parked his car and was wandering around looking for the big red house at the edge of the city. He had a wallet full of money which he flashed under the startled farmworker's nose, and no idea of where he was or where he came from. He gave his name as that of a well known comedian, which made me think he was making it up. In fact, that was the one thing he was sure of.

I phoned in and waited for the patrol car to arrive. Meanwhile, the main problem was keeping the old gentleman in one place! He kept roaming off, muttering under his breath. I was not very comfortable with him, being unsure of his reactions and unaware of how I could keep him if he insisted on leaving.

Eventually the patrol car came into the drive, and a very kind PC talked quietly to the old man, calming his fears, in direct contrast to the doctor, who was brusque and almost brutal in his approach to what turned out to be a case of senility. Someone had put the old man in his car, pointed him in the right direction and let matters take their course.

In our first year there was the tiny boy who had taken

something from the local Post Office and was refusing to repent. His father brought him along, clutching his teddy bear with tears spilling down his cheeks. Outside in the car were his pyjamas in case he had to spend the night in gaol. My heart melted but with great seriousness John took the child into the office and shut the door. I heard him say, "You just have to tell the truth, I only put liars in gaol." The little lad left, subdued but tearless and to my knowledge never got into trouble again.

No Kidding

When we first moved to Wyford we made two very special small friends – Jason, who was just mobile and Becky, a black-browed, solemn little girl of two-and-a-half. The children were the youngest in the road and once they conquered their initial shyness with us the constant stream of baby animals that appeared over the fence proved to be an irresistible attraction. They toddled behind us at feeding times, scattering corn, holding bottles and picking up eggs. Their parents might talk about John the policeman but to them he was the man who never minded letting them play with the lambs and who smiled at their childish confidences.

One evening as we were getting ready to go out there was a knock at the front door. When John answered it he found two diminutive poachers, Jason aged three and Becky four-and-a-half, together with a fishy parcel they had caught with a pin and some bread and jam. Taking it home to show Mum the harassed and later embarrassed lady had muttered, "Perhaps Mr. Bryant will buy it from you." (Mr. Bryant being a man who came round in his car delivering groceries.) The enterprising pair misheard and decided to sell it to Mr. Wyeth for his tea – no hand-outs here for the local constabulary. They were equally vague about the Trade Descriptions Act, convinced their minute fish was a trout. John managed to keep a straight face while refusing this tasty morsel, but later was unable to resist regaling their parents with the story. The youngsters never lived it down.

There is nothing like glimpsing a child's eye view of the world. Whenever John talked to the local primary school they were avid for blood and thunder. Had he ever shot anyone or hit a man with his truncheon? Who has he killed? What about bank robbers? Despite the lack of bodies or wounds the children seem to lap it up. After one talk an eight-year-old girl confessed in an essay she wanted to be a police worm when she grew up. Ah well!

Now it was time to concentrate on kids of the four-legged variety. When the time came to mate the nannies I watched for signs of wetness or redness under the tail. This, together with frantic tail wagging and loud bleating, heralds when a goat is in season. This happens for three days every three weeks and continues from autumn to spring.

A common fallacy is that goats are smelly creatures, the reason being that during the rut the billy has a strong, musky, all-pervading odour. Mating involves a great deal of foreplay, sniffing and licking, but the actual mounting is over in seconds and it can be difficult to decide if penetration has occurred. The billy throws his head back at the moment of ejaculation, a sign to watch for.

Snoopy, after a journey in the trailer, was never very co-operative. Imagine the scene: the eager billy with his watchful and protective owner, determined he shall not get overstressed; the reluctant nanny with her embarrassed and apologetic handler, coaxing and wheedling. Poor John at Snoopy's head while she took evasive action, the amorous billy jumping all over him to get to his intended mate, liberally dousing all in the vicinity with a smell that lingers in the nostrils for hours and the clothes for months. At last the deed was done and we settled down to wait five months for Snoopy's first kidding.

She decided to give birth in the hot noonday sun in a patch of nettles, ignoring the cool stable with its clean bedding. I stayed with her as she ground her teeth and the contractions began, talking soothingly and waiting for the birth.

In swift succession three black and white nanny kids were born, all perfect. Within an hour they were on their feet, unsteadily gazing at the world through amber eyes, searching for the teats with tiny head butts and madly wagging tails.

Snoopy, in her usual stubborn way, would only allow one kid to suckle, so it was bottle-feeding for months. The first twenty-four hours are vital to new-born animals; with their mother's first milk they take the colostrum that will protect them in their early days. So the milk had to be eased from Snoopy's bulging udder and placed in bottles for the kids. Like all bottle-fed animals the kids were used to being handled from birth and were very tame and confident with people.

At first glance all the kids looked exactly alike, but closer scrutiny revealed differences. The first-born had decorative tassels which many goats have. In this case instead of on the neck, as is usual, they were under her ears, like tiny earrings. We called her Tassy.

The second kid had a large patch on her side – we named her Pretty. The third baby was to go to another goatkeeper who called her Mandy. This was the only kid Snoopy paid any attention to. She was not a good mother, answering her babies' cries only if they were shrill enough, ignoring them for the most part. The kids were self-sufficient, huddling together with bodies touching. Beginning games instinctively they would leap up and race around the pen as if of one mind.

Two goats were more than enough for our needs but I so wanted to keep one of Snoopy's kids. John made all the right noises – we hadn't room, we couldn't afford a third goat, definitely not! Eventually the choice was made for us: I had settled on Pretty to keep, but Tassy chose us. She would jump onto our laps in the sunshine, constantly demanding our attention. When the time came to part she was already in our hearts so Pretty went to a new home, carefully vetted by us and Tassy remained to delight us with her affection. She lived with us for more than fifteen years, dying of old age in the same spot where she was born.

Dear Sir or Policemans Wife

My first encounter with Ronald was one I am unlikely to forget. I opened the door to a huge man – unshaven, dark-skinned and stuttering – who loomed in the doorway asking to speak to PC Wyeth.

John had met Ronald and his family as he patrolled his rural beat. Ronald rode a moped with L plates in total disregard for the formalities of which he was ignorant. He is retarded but his logic and vocabulary are astonishing. He once asked me, "Why are people so interested in Corfe Castle? Corfe Castle is a derelict building!" Try explaining that!

For most of his thirty-six years Ronald had lived away from people with his elderly parents. His father was a farm worker, nicknamed Piggery Pete, who took his son out and gave him jobs to do which kept Ronald happily occupied. He would then take Ronald to the pub and buy him a pint of lemonade.

After Pete's death the problems began. Suddenly Ronald was deprived of the only male companionship he had ever known, and as neither he nor his mother could drive legitimately they were constantly in each other's company in their remote house on the edge of Salisbury Plain.

This is when Ronald began to call at the Police Station. The policeman was his friend and a source of meeting the inarticulated needs that he was only dimly aware of. Whenever he and his mother had a quarrel he would arrive on the doorstep demanding that John sort things out. If I was alone he would frown at me and ask, "Is anybody there?"

"Yes, I am."

"Is P.C. Wyeth there?"

"No, he's at work, can I help?"

"But it's Sunday!"

"He works some Sundays."

"But it's dinner time!"

"He's had his dinner."

"But his car is here!"

"He is in the police van!"

Ronald's requests were modest: would John ask so and so, usually young men of about twenty, to be his friend, and would he find somewhere for him to play pool and skittles. These were the things that the young men Ronald wished to emulate did – they represented the society he craved.

The Police Club had recently installed a skittle alley. We took him there one morning and he skittled to his heart's content and wasn't half bad. He bought a 'white lemonade' as he used to when his father took him to the pub and went home satisfied.

On or off duty callers are always dealt with – an integral part of a community policeman's life and one reason why many officers were reluctant to move to a country station, preferring to finish work at the end of their shift. In towns the local policeman, doctor or vicar can go through the motions; in a village more is expected. The job is a whole way of life, and the role can never be shaken off.

I got used to finding all manner of waifs and strays, human and animal, on the doorstep, and inevitably would invite them in while I called John to return to the office. One night around 10.30 the caller was a very frightened young man being chased because he owed money. He had cowered under our oil tank while his

pursuers searched the area, and, certain they would break his legs if he returned home without a police escort, stood crestfallen and very damp in the pouring rain.

Frantic knocking at the front door obviously heralded an emergency. I opened it to discover a small boy – grubby faced and trembling, in desperate distress. He had gone fishing in the early morning to a spot he knew was out of bounds. While he was about his nefarious business a passer-by spotted his brand new bike in the hedge. Seeing no one around he assumed it had been stolen and dumped, so he put it in the back of his car and handed it to us as found property. The poor little chap returned empty-handed to find his prize possession gone. Convinced divine retribution had struck because he had been poaching he turned up at our door in floods of tears to confess. He left considerably chastened and convinced that crime doesn't pay.

One elderly spinster came because she was convinced that aliens had landed. Taken aback I asked how she knew – only to be told that car drivers on the A36 were signalling to her by dipping their lights as they passed. As it was a very dark night and a busy road I concluded I was unlikely to meet little green men in Wyford that evening.

Another doorstep offering was a brood of eight delightful baby ducklings, spilling out of a basket. The lady had found them by the road, scooped them up and delivered them to us. John had been nicknamed 'the good life policeman', and once people realized we had animals they were even more inclined to bring livestock to hand in. Unfortunately we've yet to have a pig or a heifer,

something really useful! In this instance the mother duck was probably close by and would have returned to her offspring if they had been left alone. As it was the orphans were left in the spare bedroom overnight and by the morning they had tumbled down the stairs and were quacking cheerfully all over the house.

I once gave tea to a pair of runaways who turned up shivering and despondent one cold afternoon. The two twelve year-old urchins had gone walkabout from their Bristol homes for a country adventure, and found it not to their taste – unlike the home-made cakes when they gave themselves up!

They were returned home, courtesy of various Police Forces – delivered in relays across force boundaries and returned to the metropolis from whence they came.

I still treasure the priceless thankyou letter they sent – addressed to 'The Policeman's Wife. Wyford Police Station.'

It read:

Dear Sir or Policemans Wife ?
Just a note to say thank you for your kindness
Saturday evening. We were taken to the main road
just outside town and just as it began to rain we
got a lift all the way to the centre of Bristol, we
were home by eleven o'clock where we had a bath
and a long sleep.
 Thank you very much for the food and kindness,
 Chris R. and Chris M.
PS The policeman who gave us the lift said you
were 'too soft' and he wouldn't have given us
anything. But we were greatful as we were really
hungry.
 Thanks.

My contribution to youthful public relations may have been
limited to baby animals, cakes and sympathy, John had an even
more appealing angle. Six year-old Jonathan had for more than
two-thirds of his life had a police career in mind. Hero worship
set in from the time my husband first called at his home in
uniform. He was a joyous child, bright, and impossible to resist
or ignore. One wondrous day, washed and scrubbed, his play police
helmet on his head, miniature handcuffs in his pocket, he sat
proud as a peacock in the passenger seat of the police van for a
ride along the private farm track where he lives. He saw how the
radio worked and the blue light flashed just for him, a great
adventure for one very excited little boy. At one time most children
would know their local policeman and relationships of trust and
respect were built up from their earliest years. Many are the tales
of the village bobbies told by local residents who recall with
affection being caught scrumping or riding bikes without lights,
and how the law dealt with them – usually with a clip around the
ear with the parents' blessing.
 In a modern age this continuity has been interrupted; only in
isolated pockets are rural police stations still operating. Here a

generation of children have grown up knowing their local policeman – he has talked to them in class, helped build their play areas, passed the time of day with them at dances, stopped them for speeding and signed their passports. They produce their documents with no sign of ill-feeling and ask for advice without hesitation.

I have been lucky in that, of necessity, I have been involved with John's work in a way that would never have been possible if we hadn't moved to Wyford. I have coped with many odd events. Even so, the evening my husband deposited a black plastic bin liner in the office for the weekend I eyed it with considerable misgiving. "What are you planning to do with that?" I asked, as if I didn't know!

I had put up with poachers' ill gotten gains reposing for months in the freezer, hand grenades handed in casually at the front door and a family of ducklings let loose all over the house. We had had a stolen car on the front lawn in imminent danger of being petrol bombed by thieves who had returned to destroy the evidence, made a Molotov cocktail from a milk bottle and set its companion alight, a circumstance guaranteed to make sleep impossible once I was aware of it.

Human remains in the office was quite another thing. There had been a bit of a flap the week before when a soldier on a military exercise had discovered part of a skeleton while digging a trench. At first no one was sure if a relatively recent murder had been unearthed. However it proved to be an ancient burial and all was left so that archaeologists from Salisbury Museum could examine the site to see if it had any significance.

Until now the bones had stayed in John's van but, as he had the weekend off and the van was needed, a new resting place was necessary until the experts arrived on Tuesday. The remains lay on the floor of the office and I gave them a wide berth, my imagination working overtime in the dark hours.

John was not on duty when he guided the archaeologists to the remote part of Salisbury Plain where the discovery was made, so I was able to go along. They found at least three bodies buried, a male skeleton on its side, and a female with a child laying on her breast. Whether there were any more bodies beneath the chalk was anyone's guess. The fact that no artifacts were found meant that the burial was possibly Christian, maybe as far back as the Roman Occupation. With the multitude of ancient sites Wiltshire possesses it was deemed not worth excavating, so the trench was filled in and the lonely spot was left to disappear once more beneath the rough grasses and lowering skies of the prehistoric landscape.

Herbie

Several years into backyarding I attended a course of self-sufficiency lectures at Lackham Agricultural College. Listening to the one on goatkeeping, all the do's and dont's made me grateful for Jill Russell's sensible advice. I wondered if, had realized at the beginning all that the experts say is entailed, I would have had the courage to start. Being a country policeman's wife was very much the same in many ways!

For the goats the necessary basics are a draught-proof shelter with plenty of room if the goats need to be shut in in bad weather and adequate drainage. A dirt floor with deep layers of straw is the easiest bedding; this has the added advantage of only needing mucking out three times a year as the seasons change. Clean bedding strewn on top of old ensures a build up of heat for the bitter weather and keeps the animals comfortable. A reasonably high ceiling is important or the goatkeeper has to bend over double as the layers build up.

Escape-proof fencing is a must if you wish to preserve your marriage and your sanity. Goats are great escapers and the forbidden is irresistible: they will find any weak spot and squeeze through. Fence posts and wire make life much pleasanter.

We have these days a large, corrugated garage which has one stall containing hay and straw, a second for kidding and a large loose box area. A salt lick and a bucket of fresh water provide the essentials. Goats are very pernickety eaters. If hay falls on the floor out of indoor mangers and gets trodden on it is no use for feed; if it is replaced in the hay rack they will ignore it. Large gaps in mangers are to be avoided – the animal will pull out more than it wants and waste half.

We take our goats to a small enclosed field on fine days to graze, this gives a welcome change of scene and a more varied diet. Their shed leads on to a run; during bad weather they are left at home with the bottom half of their door open so they can be in or out as they choose.

Tethers are not a good idea on a permanent basis though they are ideal if a small piece of ground needs clearing. Young kids should never be tethered: they leap and twist and are liable to damage themselves if left unattended. Goats hate to get wet, fussing loudly if they are chained and unable to get to shelter. Contrarily, if they are free to seek it they may decide to eat out anyway. They browse rather than graze, picking at a variety of foliage. It took a while to get used to watching them demolish nettles, rose bushes and thorns and all with evident relish.

Nannies need concentrates daily, fresh greens and a good supply of good quality hay.

Worming needs to be done, so does hoof-trimming. Goats' hooves grow as our nails do and can become ingrown making the animal hobble. A sharp knife and a steady hand are all that are needed. I stand at the animal's head and hold her collar while John wields the knife or the hoof trimmers, paring the overgrown hoof away. It doesn't hurt and for the most part the goats bear with us patiently.

One thing the Russells impressed on us before they let us have Snoopy was the necessity of accepting that billy kids are meat animals. Only a few of the very best bred kids become stud billies, pampered and cared for, never overtaxed and much sought after to improve the stock of other goatkeepers. With goat multiple births the percentage of males is high. They are adorable babies but grow large, needing food and shelter, seasonally smelly and, if they are left alone, are prone to wander.

Goats are agile creatures and can clear fences with ease for the most part. Billies need very secure penning. They will never be productive and are totally useless to most households, besides being immensely strong and difficult to control in many cases. Even nannies are subject to ill-treatment and neglect, the fate of billy kids bought in a misguided sentimental moment is likely to be horrific as they reach maturity.

Some goatkeepers put billy kids down at birth, I have never found the heart to kill a brand new baby animal, but this is by far the kindest thing to do if in the next four months you are likely to allow sentiment to overcome sense. Selling at markets to escape responsibility for the kid's death can mean the animal ends up in a laboratory or is killed inhumanely to satisfy alien dietary codes. Caring goatkeepers never sell where the animal goes to the highest bidder. We advertise, then check prospective owners. People new to goatkeeping should ensure they understand what is required to keep the goat happy. Far better the animal goes for meat, and is properly killed than sent to a home where it will not be valued and may be ill-treated.

Herbie was a perfect example. He was taken to a goat rescue service after spending his first three years of life in a Bristol back garden. He was small, friendly and unquestionably the smelliest animal I have ever encountered. He spent a month with friends of ours so that he could serve their two nannies and our Tassy. None of us had more than a passing acquaintance with billies, so we were unprepared for how anti-social a billy goat can be. The clothes the men wore to lead him through the village needed immediate washing, even the flash-light they carried stank so badly it was banished outside for days to eradicate the pong.

Herbie had never had access to his own kind; he had previously spent some time at the Russells and became used to their sheep.

In the field next to his new hosts was a ram. Herbie decided to join him; he barged through and over fences leaving destruction in his wake. He was secure enough as long as there was someone at home to keep an eye on him, but when the family were at work they dared not leave him in the field. It bordered on several well-stocked back gardens and the ado likely to arise if their owners had to evict a smelly, stubborn billy goat was not to be contemplated. This meant Herbie had to be shut in a stall, which became extremely messy and very fetid. Herbie had a habit of urinating on himself and in a confined space his personal hygiene was less than satisfactory. Keeping Herbie proved a lesson well learned by all who came near him, and his reluctant hosts heaved a sigh of relief when he returned whence he came.

Horns are another problem that need to be dealt with after kidding. Popular myth has it that all goats have horns. In fact many are hornless – a bald nanny like Snoopy and a horned male produced one hornless and two horned kids. When they're born the babies have two tiny swirls like kiss curls on their heads if they are going to have horns. After a couple of days these can be felt coming through.

Most goatkeepers today have the kids disbudded if they are not going for meat, a job that needs to be done at ten days-old by a vet. This is necessary for safety. In a herd environment where there are several goats together they will play, mock joust and sometimes, when a newcomer is introduced, they will fight. Horned animals can do their stable mates a great deal of damage; their owners too – a quick toss of the head can result in a nasty accident.

Goathorn is surprisingly strong. The base is very large, especially on kids with their small skulls. When Snoopy's kids were born we had our first veterinary experience – Mandy and Tassy needed disbudding. We took the kids, bursting with energy, and drove fifteen miles to the vet's surgery. At the reception the girls were all very taken with the babes. Over the years it has always impressed me how caring the whole practice is with animals. A lot of group practice doctors could learn from our vet.

We were told to return in half-an-hour. Mandy and Tassy were woozy from the anaesthetic and they had two huge patches on their foreheads where the horn had been burnt out. I was horrified but assured that as soon as the sedatives wore off they would be as right as rain and show no sign of distress. They slept on my lap on the car journey home and within an hour were their normal, bouncy selves.

The next time we had to take a kid to be disbudded the vet, with whom we were on good terms, allowed us into the surgery to watch the operation. That year we had Rudy and his sister Juby (born in Jubilee year). As the twins were never parted we decided the experience would be less traumatic for Juby if Rudy was nearby. The only time she screamed was when Rudy was out of her sight. I moved nearer the table, the baby was injected and when the hot tongs were applied to her head Juby never even flinched. After that I felt much happier about the process.

As with everything else there was a lot to learn about goatkeeping. The costs are not great and in non-financial terms the rewards are enormous, but it proved a commitment not to be made lightly.

Country Coppering

O ur second year at Wyford was marked by a visit from the Chief Superintendent of the Division. These were yearly inspections and interviews to check that all was running smoothly and gave the officer the opportunity to make comments or complaints as he saw fit.

This particular spring our pigsty was in the process of being built. In our early years, economy won out over beauty; to uninitiated eyes our animal complex may have appeared a little ramshackle!

The Police Superintendent spotted our latest architectural venture and queried if we had planning permission, something which we had never considered. In the event it was not necessary for the local authority, though the Police Authority was another matter.

It dawned on me that if the powers that be said no we would have to dismantle the goat shed as well, then where would our pets live? We were fortunate in that the Chief Superintendent was sympathetic to our needs and wrote in his report that PC Wyeth had succumbed to an innocuous country habit; his support was noted and permission to continue granted.

One of the girl cadets stationed in the town at the time used to complain that every time she had to see the Chief Constable he would ask about PC Wyeth and his pigs! After five years and in the midst of redecoration and a heavy snowfall he came to see for himself, together with Her Majesty's Inspector and various other officials.

John's immediate bosses had talked to him beforehand, a mini-briefing to ensure all went smoothly. All this for nothing; after three questions on general police work HMI wanted to talk about carrots, and everyone took off around the garden to inspect the livestock. The visit seemed to go well; at least it was different, and we were left in peace.

Country folk retain the old values – a spirit of cooperation and unity evident – and woe betide the town crook caught about his nefarious business by the locals.

A rural sub Post Office was broken into one night and the neighbours, hearing a disturbance, dialled 999. They then raised the village. By the time John arrived the place was surrounded by men with pitchforks, staffs and shotguns. The thief, discovered cowering in the loft, was profoundly relieved to be taken into custody.

Another time while John was patrolling he

spotted a car that had been circulated that morning as having failed to stop for an officer in another county. He followed it and the three occupants – two men and a woman, seeing they had been recognized, took off into alien countryside.

They approached a sharp bend on the back road at speed and with last minute and fatal decision went straight ahead up a track which was almost knee-deep in mud. Their car stuck fast; they abandoned it and took to their heels, with our helmeted hero in hot pursuit.

At the top of the lane there was a fork. One man made his escape across the field towards a hamlet while the others ran along the track which only led deeper into the rural fastness.

After a mad scramble across field and fence the lone man was caught and handcuffed over the chevron sign at the bend in the road to the delight of the policemen who, responding to a call for assistance, were greeted first by the offenders rear end as they erupted round the corner.

Meanwhile local farmworkers had come along and, on being appraised of the situation, began with their vehicles and CB radios to search the wooded hillsides for the remaining absconders. Extra police officers and a dog handler were having little success when over the police radio a voice was heard speaking to the control room with information as to the whereabouts of the fugitives. The bemused station Sergeant was heard to query, "Well who are you then?"

A soft Wiltshire accent replied, "John Wyeth knows me."

The farmworker was using the radio in John's abandoned van, firmly stuck in the mud and left unlocked in the first hectic moments of the chase. The police officers, not having CBs, could not be contacted except through their normal communication channels.

Set the scene: a townsman and woman, lost in the midst of rolling downland, far from any road or habitation, hiding in the trees. The farm manager, Bob Beagley, a huge man with a ruddy complexion and a ready sense of humour, shouts in his booming voice, "Come out ya buggers or I'll shoot!" The sorry pair stagger from the bushes, hands up and shaking. There was no weapon of any kind, but the posse had had a whale of a time and their adventure will go down in folklore for years to come.

Country coppering is seldom dull, and though most of the time John has patrolled a rural beat, over the years he has had other duties which take him away. The 1983/84 miners' strike is one example. Despite media coverage of violence there were many pits where things were less ugly and miners who wished to work were grateful for the police presence. Mining helmets, belts and snap tins were amongst the keepsakes brought home – presents from the pit workers. But it was a long year as the men were away a week at a time and wives scanned the news anxiously, living with an ever-present but mostly suppressed fear for their safety.

Fear is always part of being married into the 'job'; mostly it is buried deep in the subconscious, surfacing on rare occasions and seldom admitted to. There are dark, stormy nights when conditions are treacherous and accidents abound; police vehicles hastening to the scene are not miraculously immune. There are call-outs and times when men are hours overdue: a shift ends when the job is done, not always when the appointed eight hours have passed. Husbands do not always arrive home in the pristine condition they left in, and inevitably they are affected by the darker side of life that for most people is seen on TV but encountered infrequently in reality.

Mealtimes are not sacrosanct as any police wife will tell you, and weekends and Bank Holidays are policed as usual so that while the world is at leisure our men are elsewhere. There is no such thing as being off-duty and turning a blind eye. Our very first local dance taught me that lesson when my escort disappeared outside to calm down a potentially explosive situation. Friends need to accept that long-laid plans are subject to last minute cancellations and intimate suppers are subject to interruption.

❦

Leaving a retirement party after midnight John spotted something out of place which left him racing off into the darkness, leaving me prey to all kinds of fears. He found a man slashing tyres in the police car park; it was hours before we got to bed!

I was waiting outside when a policeman knocked on my window. "John has to take a statement because he's made an arrest. Bring the car into the car park, then you can come in and wait."

I had passed my driving test only weeks before; I was cold, tired and had lost my voice. The car park was an expanse of blackness, threatening shadows and menace. Was there only the man who had been caught, or did his companion lurk in the shadows?

The car park was full, there was just one small space, I began my manoeuvre, and as I did so I touched, oh so gently, a patrol car. Then I couldn't move! Suddenly the night erupted as policemen responded to a call. I got out, wringing my hands, "You'll have to move me, I'm afraid I've hit a police car." No such luck, I had to await the sergeant and his tape measure and make my own statement. It was a very little dent, but my first prang was in the Police Car Park at midnight!

One of the advantages of living amid the people you police is that most of the residents meet their local sheriff off-duty. Many are the quiet words in the ear which would never reach a more impersonal station.

When people are in trouble or in stressful situations, having a familiar and trusted face has a very calming effect. The day an elderly spinster with a persecution complex took to her bed because 'God told her to die' it was John who climbed a ladder to the bedroom window and convinced her God had told him she was to get up.

When a call came from a very unhappy and suicidal man it was my husband he wanted to see. John was on duty and went immediately. When his shift ended and the next day *en route* to a court appearance he took the time to check and make sure all was well. Another man in the depths of depression shut himself in and refused to eat. It was the local policeman who talked to him and arranged for his removal to hospital.

Living in a small community has many positive aspects, but knowing your neighbours means that when tragedy strikes it is far more personal, and has a very real impact. Suicides were just something I read about in the newspapers before moving to Wyford – it was a shock to find that within the area of one rural beat there were so many desperately unhappy people. I soon recognized that weekends seem to be a particularly vulnerable time – in the years at Wyford there have been drug overdoses, drownings – once by someone who put their head in a bucket of water, shotgun suicides and carbon monoxide poisoning in cars.

How often I wonder have police wives had someone say to them, "But your husband is too nice to be a policeman!" It is hard to remember that the majority of the public only sees a police officer in unpleasant circumstances, and rarely meets one socially. The image portrayed on TV of a hard drinking, swearing bully boy is a difficult one to live down. Policemen are people, and most of them are caring, humorous individuals who do their job with courage and compassion.

The Ones that Got Away

Our one attempt at keeping animals purely as pets was a disaster. I first saw Peruvian guinea pigs at a friend's house. Normal guinea pigs are too rodent-like to appeal to me, but these small creatures, with their long, silky fur, their bright eyes, button noses and tiny paws, were adorable. My friend washed their coats each week, dried them with a hair-dryer, and handled them regularly so that they were tame – ideal creatures to pet. With Snoopy growing up, these Dougal-like creatures seemed a good idea, so Clothears and Chuckletummy came to stay.

In the beginning I had them indoors each day to get used to me. They had an endearing habit of remaining absolutely motionless if they were afraid in the mistaken belief that they were invisible. As Clothears was a snowy albino and Chuckletummy was multi-coloured they were noticeable wherever they were.

It was summer, the guinea pigs living in a hutch with a moveable run. People who came to the door were hard put to decide if they were looking at puppies or the Magic Roundabout come to life. Local children admired them enviously.

One morning when I went to feed them Chuckletummy was

missing. I searched the garden with Clothears under my arm in the hope of enticing his brother out of hiding, to no avail. Tearfully, knowing he was defenceless against attack, I was sure he had made a colourful breakfast for someone's dog or cat.

Having a lonely animal was not to be thought of so, that afternoon, it was down to the pet shop where I saw Cuddlypuff, a female Peruvian who was quite beautiful. She looked as if she had a white blouse, a black waistcoat and a russet skirt. Clothears was impressed, so was Chuckletummy who promptly reappeared from beneath the woodpile, eager to return to captivity.

Now the problems began – the males fought for possession of the female, teeth chattering and leaping in the air: they were unexpectedly ferocious. When the first babies arrived we kept one female to maintain a balance, giving the rest of the little ones away. Our intention was to segregate the sexes which was easier said than done. I ran out of homes for the guinea pigs, my sexing was haphazard and this resulted in yet another population explosion in several households.

Eventually, during one very hot summer, the males succumbed to heat stroke, and when Cuddlypuff eventually gave up the ghost we gave her companion away and breathed a sigh of relief.

Bees were the one thing I refused to agree to having around. Each time I began to think maybe I could live with them the TV would rescreen films like 'The Killer Swarm' and I would change my mind again. Eventually I gave in to John's pleas and in double quick time we had a hive, a hat and gloves: all we needed was the bees.

Our first swarm arrived in the evening and seemed to go into the hive without difficulty; in our innocence we thought we were in the honey business.

The next morning two bomb disposal men arrived to collect one of the unexploded shells handed in from Salisbury Plain, then reposing in the rhubarb patch. A steady stream of bullets, shells and hand grenades regularly arrived on our doorstep, handled with casual disregard by the finders, who seemed blissfully unaware of their explosive capabilities. At least we never suffered the fate of the main Police Station, when a helpful member of the public walked in off the street with a butterfly bomb he had in the attic, having seen what it was on the TV programme 'U.X.B.' That little escapade emptied the Station, the street and the bowels of the unfortunate officer at the desk.

This morning the bees were very active and the soldiers, who are without doubt some of the bravest men in the Army, handling explosives with aplomb, were less assured when dealing with mother nature – detouring around the garden to avoid all contact with the mass of insects.

What I didn't realise was that the intense activity meant I was about to witness my first swarm. The noise grew, the air appeared black with moving specks, and the bees took off in a huge, dark cloud, disappearing over the treetops. When John arrived home for lunch he discovered his precious haul had vanished.

A few weeks later we received a call from the main Police Station – the owner of a garden in the town had complained of a swarm of bees, did we want them? One of us obviously did, so off we set on a hot afternoon. The swarm had settled in a tree; John, with a display of valour bordering on insanity, donned a hat, a veil and gloves and walked into the humming horde. Grasping the branch firmly he began to shake the tight mass of black insects into a cardboard box. The air became alive with bees, exactly like a Hammer horror movie, with our hero calmly going about his business.

Once all had quietened down the box was closed and we began the seven-mile journey home. Glancing back I saw, to my horror, that the back window was covered with bees; more and more were crawling through the gap in the box lid – we were shut in with hundreds of stinging insects! We opened all the windows, donned veils (as I was in a short-sleeved mini-dress the protection afforded was less than adequate) and drove home as fast as we dared.

Despite our efforts the swarm died, possibly due to being caught in a chemical spray before we found them. I got my first sting, on the cheek, as I walked past the car, having collected the goats from grazing. Very painful it was too, though I got little sympathy because my brunette colouring makes me less prone to swell up, unlike my fair-skinned husband. I didn't look pathetic enough which just shows there is no justice when dealing with nature!

Thankfully our third swarm did stay with us; John took the hive to the bees and returned with it on the trailer. It was fortunate we hadn't had to buy a swarm or we would have seen our money take off into the air which would have added insult to injury.

The goats have been the greatest escapers of all, in our novice days a smooth-talking local convinced us we should buy an electric fence which he assured us would keep the goats in. Of course it didn't; we would wake up to find Sherry eating the roses or the runner beans with equal relish, and Snoopy playing leapfrog on top of cloches and squashing the tender plants beneath. The kid would leap through the strands and her mother would brave the slight shock to follow. Decent fencing was the only way to contain them and retain our sanity.

Goats adore wood, they strip the bark from trees and attack wooden buildings with their teeth. When Holly first arrived our chicken shed had a hardboard side. John, returning from duty one afternoon, found Hollygoat had eaten a hole in the board and was head and almost shoulders out of the run. Speedy repairs and more substantial wood was called for.

Holly had only kidded once, in her distant youth, so when we took her to be mated we hoped for the best. In March her twins were born: like their mother they were brown and white Toggenburgs, a billy and a nanny we called Tammy.

Holly was a doting mother, anxiously attending every bleat. Tammy had one of the shrillest, most penetrating cries I have ever heard, and she was a remarkable jumper, a fact we discovered early on.

Holly's udder quickly became sore and bloody from the kids suckling, so after eight days we moved Tammy and Billy to the pigsty where we had a pair of lambs ensconced. Pudding and Noisy were the same age, all the babies were bottle-fed and the sty quickly became known as the nursery.

When the kids were two weeks-old John took his Venture Scouts to Sweden for Easter, leaving me literally holding the babies. The midnight feed meant I had four eager, wriggling animals crowding at the gate in the darkness to be fed. On my own, it was difficult to keep track of where all the tinies were, the simplest way was to reach over the fence and lift them out one at a time.

Tammy discovered food was over the fence and she didn't need me to help her overcome such an obstacle. At four weeks-old she was clearing a four-foot fence with ease. John returned, raised the fence and we relaxed.

The pigsty building and the goatshed adjoined – Tammy would leap onto the roof of the sty, then onto the higher stable roof, skip and cavort before leaping into the goat run and over the lower, more permanent fence there.

Her brother couldn't follow her example, and in the perverse manner that marked her early on, the moment freedom was achieved she objected to the loneliness and wanted company. Her intelligence never seemed to go into reverse, and while she was perfectly capable of gaining her objective to get out, she never worked out how to get back in again. The night would be rent with her excruciating screams for attention. We would respond, restore her to her playmates, whereupon in five minutes she was out again and the whole charade would begin anew.

The animals' pens looked more like Colditz every day, yet still she managed to escape. Eventually we had to resort to either shutting her in the shed or chaining her up. The chain was successful as long as her playmates stayed close by, but if they moved out of sight the screaming would begin, and go on and on and on until we were completely demoralized.

When we went out for the day we took all the babies to a friend so that they could be fed. On our return we learned that Tammy had escaped from a field, a tether and a potting shed – somehow she had wriggled through a small window high in the shed wall. Every time we left the house we feared what we would find on our return. Eventually we asked her new owners if they would take her early, having warned them of her leaping ability. They had a proper stable where she was less likely to escape. She managed to catch her neck in the manger one night and was dead in the morning, Tammy's short, eventful life had lasted just six months.

Pigs at the Poky

Noisy and Pudding were our first two lambs. They had a disastrous habit, once away from our watchful care, of wandering off. After six weeks of living in the garden, they were put to graze in a village a mile away where they had the run of the orchard. The fencing had been especially erected to hold two small and adventurous lambs, yet still they managed to find any weak spot – every gap in the hedge – or to wriggle beneath the electric fence.

The only things that mattered in the neglected garden were the roses and a foreign vine, lovingly tended. They stripped the vine as far up as they could reach and ate the roses with relish. We would get phone calls to say our lambs had gone walkabout through the village, and would have to drop everything to round them up.

The owners of the orchard, an American racing driver and his English wife, were often abroad. Their house was remote from the rest of the village and they were glad to have someone calling in regularly. The wife, a well connected young woman, was at the airport one day, talking to a friend at an airline desk. She commented that it was useful to have her local policeman keeping sheep in her garden.

Somehow one of the gossip columnists picked up the story,

and in William Hickey's column the story appeared. No names or locations were mentioned, just that a certain someone had a unique crime deterrent in the form of her local policeman's flock of sheep.

The Chief Constable of the time made enquiries, the main concern being the word 'flock'; were we in the sheep-rearing business? Within the Police Force any business interests are declared and mainly forbidden: we were thankful we could set the record straight.

Later that same year the house was broken into, although nothing was taken. In the course of time some men were caught and charged with various offences. Among the crimes they admitted was the forced entry to the racing driver's house. While they were inside they heard movements in the orchard, so left empty-handed. The lambs had inadvertently saved the day, not to mention the TV and the silver!

Our first two pigs were no problem and we were lured into a false sense of security. The next three were less amenable. The moment I went into the sty with their food they would try and get out of the gate; if they succeeded they usually returned easily enough for their food but inevitably the day arrived when one of the pigs was less tempted by the contents of the trough than by the cabbage patch.

I grasped a trotter and pulled. The pig squealed and writhed, we got nowhere. Pigs are notoriously difficult animals to catch hold of – they are large, strong and close enough to the ground that your balance is overset from the start. They have no necks to speak of, while neither ears nor tails are satisfactory handles to grasp. I well recall the day John and I were walking past the local pig farm when a mass breakout took place.

The pigs were huge and in a hurry. I stood, arms akimbo, intending to remain steady – bravery succumbed to cowardice when they kept coming and I dived for cover.

John, who is made of sterner stuff, grabbed a tail. Round and round the yard the pig charged, John hanging on for dear life, his attempts to stop having no noticeable effect on the pig's mobility.

Back at the Police Station panic was setting in as I grappled with an animal as determined as me but with more muscle power. Help came in the surprising form of an elderly Polish lady who had kept pigs in the old country. With her aid and at her suggestion I made a noose of bailer twine from the hay bales, which I put around the pig's leg. With two of us pushing and shoving the errant porker eventually returned whence he came.

Then there was Snuffles. All the while we had kept pink pigs I had gazed with admiration and envy at the beautiful marmalade-coloured Tamworths that are bred nearby. One afternoon we received a phone call from the farm – there was a Tamworth runt to be disposed of, were we interested? I was unsure whether we should have a solitary pig but the opportunity was too rare and too wonderful to resist.

John had been working on the trailer, it still needed work but we foresaw no problems in carrying one tiny piglet. We first collected some bales of straw to keep out draughts in the sty and make a deep nest for our new baby's bedding, then drove to the farm.

At first sight Snuffles was so small, only a third of the size of the rest of the pen. I always overlook how tiny piglets are in the beginning and how fast they grow.

The runt was caught and carried protesting to the trailer. We stood back to admire. She leapt on the straw and, using the bales as steps, was out of the trailer within seconds and running back to her brothers and sisters. Catching her again wasn't too difficult: we repositioned the bales and set off for home.

At the edge of Wyford a set of temporary traffic lights was showing red. We stopped and I got out to check the piglet which promptly leapt onto the bales, over the front of the trailer, making an ungainly landing but unhurt and took off up the bank.

John left the driver's seat and together we chased one small, slippery orange piglet up and down the A36, while other motorists watched open-mouthed and amused at the impromptu roadshow. Eventually surrounded and subdued, Snuffles finished the journey in the car.

She proved a very special animal, settling into life alone with no obvious discomfort. She quickly became tame and grew on her diet of weaner meal, scraps and goats' milk. I would sometimes let her into the goat run, she would race round after me, round and round my ankles, then off to scatter chickens, returning to have her back rubbed and be petted.

Despite the warnings I was unable to resist falling in love with her. She snuffled happily at the sound of my voice and became the focal point for visitors. Eventually the inevitable happened: without major reconstruction the sty was not strong or large enough for a fully grown sow and the feed bills were growing. She had always been, as my husband was fond of inelegantly reminding me, 'food on four legs'.

In the past, moving pigs had been a matter of brawn; the awful part about Snuffles departure was her trust. She allowed the rope halter to be put on and followed us unhesitatingly. Getting her into the trailer was more of an effort; pigs like to see through things and have little inclination to enter an enclosed space.

John ended up with a scraped arm on the trailer floor accompanied by160 pounds of prostrate and protesting pig. With the memory of her first journey we left the harness on and attached it to the tow-bar, visions of a marmalade porker landing on the bonnet of an unsuspecting motorist travelling behind us being too vivid to be ignored.

I cried for the first time since the early days about parting with a meat animal, and would gladly have forgotten common sense and returned with Snuffles but it was never really an option. I was left wondering if the pleasure of keeping animals can compensate for the pain of parting. Looking back I know it does.

Disasters by the Dozen

In the spring sunshine life seems idyllic – small woolly lambs play on the lawn, skipping and leaping in sheer high spirits. Fluffy yellow chicks follow their mother as she scratches for food, cheeping and scurrying under her protective wings when an intruder comes close. The goats, with entrancing kids at heel, chew the cud and accept titbits from eager hands. To a visitor on such a day our life is much to be envied. The quality of living is rich indeed, but it isn't all sunshine and sweet baby animals, it's sometimes mud, frustration and heartache.

Our early attempts at backyarding were problem-free, I realize now. Our first sitting of eggs hatched and the chicks grew to maturity, our original lambs were bottle-fed and healthy and our pigs were unbelievably easy to raise.

John had with great persistence convinced me to give pigs a chance. I was indoctrinated with the idea that they would be smelly and anti-social. In fact, of all the animals the pigs are the least bother and the most profitable: all they require is draught-proof housing, lots of straw for bedding, a small outside run and weaner mix, bought in to combine with household scraps for feed.

Our first so-called weaners were bought from an intensive pig breeding unit nearby. While the people who worked there were very caring of their charges, we were certain the pigs enjoyed a better quality of life with us. They were able to sunbathe, to root in the vegetable patch with gusto, taking as much pleasure in the nettles as they did in last year's carrots and parsnips, and exhibiting a sensual enjoyment of the cool showers from the garden hose on hot summer days.

They loved to toss the deep straw, making nests and squealing with excitement. They were petted, given a wide variety of food with plenty of milk from our surplus, and they had no need to compete with a pen-full of others at feeding times.

Our second lot of pigs, three in number, were so alike that individual names were impractical; collectively they were known as the 'Plods.' As new arrivals they were shy, racing to hide in a corner, trembling when approached but later, with familiarity, they became inquisitive, liable to shove a swilly snout against our knees in a bid for attention. This was unnerving as they got older – their massive jaws just a little too close for comfort

John's bright idea to see how much they weighed was for me to stand on the bathroom scales holding a pig, then we would

subtract my weight. Easier said than done, the pigs wriggled and screamed, there was no way I could hold them steady enough to get a reading!

The piglets would arrive just after they were weaned, at six to eight weeks, and by twenty weeks they were 120 pounds live weight. The time of parting was almost upon us when I went to feed them one cool morning. To my horror the largest of the pigs seemed to have contracted some kind of debilitating disease: he came at my call but seemed to have lost the use of his back legs. Visions of pig polio raced through my mind as I made a hurried phone call to a local pig farmer.

When the farmer arrived he was of the opinion that, as the pigs were becoming more sexually aware they had engaged in strenuous play, and an inherent weakness in the back legs had caused the damage. He was sure the meat would be alright but it was important that the animals be slaughtered swiftly or it was possible the meat would be condemned. On this occasion we were lucky but it brought home to us that nothing can be taken for granted as far as livestock is concerned.

Lambs are very prone to die at an early age when they are being hand-reared, often with no warning. My first black lamb I called Goliath, Golly for short; he was alone so he had my undivided attention. I petted and played with him, ignoring John's teasing that I should stop playing with his dinner. In the manner of bottle-fed lambs Golly would suck at the knees of my jeans, butting with his tiny, curly head, wagging his tail enthusiastically. Then, at sixteen days-old, for no obvious reason, he was dead. I was devastated.

For months things moved along smoothly, then problems crowded in thick and fast. One year we had an unprecedented succession of disasters, yet May began well enough.

We had five lambs, Caesar and Cleopatra, almost weaned and ready to leave the garden and go out to graze; Solomon whose sister Salome had been that year's casualty, and Samson and Sheba, seven days-old and newly arrived.

Sheba's beauty was marred by tiny wort-like growths over her black face. It wasn't until a neighbouring farm manager saw her that we had ever heard of Orf. Apparently a contagious disease that can in extreme cases be caught by humans, we wasted no time. The lambs were bundled in the car and off to the vet with dispatch. This time we were lucky, it was a mild form of Orf and a spray was all that was necessary to effect a cure. For weeks afterwards I examined my face in the mirror, waiting for monstrous growths to appear.

One constant irritation that particular year was the number of swarms of bees that seemed to home in on us. I had by now a working knowledge of beekeeping, but the practicalities I leave to my braver half.

Bright, warm spring weather encourages swarming and bees are attracted to gardens where there are established colonies. The flowering current and the gooseberry bushes are favourite resting places, which means the bushes are often mutilated as the branches are cut off to shake the bees into their box.

First the bees become very active, then a loud humming fills the air and the garden fills with thousands of insects; at first these cover a wide area but gradually they begin to become more concentrated. The queen bee settles on a branch or a post and slowly the moving black mass grows around her as the bees surround their Queen with a protective shield. All becomes quiet while the scouts search out a dark place to inhabit. This done, with one accord the bees again take to the air and disappear in a dark cloud.

In one nine-day period in May disasters came as thick and fast as a swarm of bees.

Day One and the owners of Wyford's soon-to-be-opened Fish and Chip shop discover bees in their cavity wall. There was no way to get to the Queen bee so the swarm had to be destroyed. It was a case of 'Let's ask John the Policeman.'

Off-duty, John donned his gear and set off to oblige the shop owners. The bees were understandably annoyed: one got under his veil and stung him at the top of his nose by his left eye. By the time he returned home he was beginning to swell and his eye was shut.

Day Two: in the midst of lunch preparations a neighbour calls to say they have a swarm in their hedge. Once more our hero gets kitted up to save the village from the humming hordes, collecting them in a box which he left in the rose bed.

That evening there was a barn dance, John went along looking like Quasimodo – being fair-skinned he always reacts alarmingly when stung.

After the dance we were invited by friends for a late supper, arriving home as the sun was rising and the dawn chorus in full song. 4.30am and unable to let well alone John checked the bees before going to bed, resulting in another sting on the left side of the jaw. As I pulled out the poison sac I wondered aloud if beekeeping as a hobby was all it was cracked up to be.

Day Three: after three hours' sleep the phone rang, it was Mr. Jackson who owned the pasture where the lambs were. Cleopatra had been chased by a dog and in heedless panic had plunged into the river, swum across to the opposite bank, returning in response to her brother's pitiful bleats. We found her damp but undaunted, a sodden fleece in the morning sunshine.

In later months the scenario was repeated, this time Cleopatra was carried downstream by the swiftly moving current. Two things conspired to save her life: Mr. Jackson witnessed the incident and ran along the bank, and the fact that upstream someone had been cutting weed. The weeds were thickly entangled beneath the footbridge and the water level was abnormally high. Mr. Jackson was able to reach down and pluck Cleopatra from her watery element as she struggled valiantly, caught in the debris.

Our bees swarmed twice that afternoon.

Day Seven: just as we were about to leave for our annual visit to relatives in Sussex, Holly goat, our old walking hearth-rug, decided to begin kidding, later than scheduled but spot on the moment we left the house. We delayed, made her comfortable and waited. The single kid – a minute and fluffy nanny – was adorable.

Tassy had produced two billies that season, and Snoopy had managed not to get pregnant at all. She had disgraced us over the years with her extreme reluctance to be mated – butting, kicking and sitting down while a succession of handsome billies had tried to woo her. Owners of pedigree stud goats are very careful, they never overtax the male's strength and carefully supervise all matings. Catching the nanny at the right moment is essential; an appointment is set up, the animals transported and then it's up to the goats. Snoopy's lack of enthusiasm in the face of rampant lust has caused human passions to flare!

Day Nine: John went to check on our newest arrival and found her dead. Holly had lain on the baby in the night, having apparently successfully given birth with no seeming complications, she had suddenly sickened.

Holly's advent into our orbit six years before as a companion for Snoopy had been fraught with difficulties. Once she had settled in she had been the boss of the goat run, nipping errant kids and butting when necessary to keep order. She was very gentle with people and a touchingly concerned mother. After so long without babies, she had her first after we took her in and she adored her offspring. If we picked them up she would shove her nose between us to make sure that all was well.

During the preceding winter she had slowed down a lot, beginning to show her age: this was to have been her last kidding. Now she was unable to understand why her baby wasn't where she left it. She wandered around the run, crying heartbreakingly.

At fourteen she had had a good life and it was time to say goodbye. Holly was the first non-meat animal we had to play God to; lambs, billy kids and pigs are all destined for food, but nanny goats are family. At least Holly died at home where she was loved and secure.

After this chapter of accidents life once more became routine, the sun continued to shine and after a while another goat took Holly's place in the garden.

Fowl Play

Nothing concentrates the mind in the early morning like the sound of a shotgun blast beneath the bedroom window, I can testify to that. It took only seconds to register in our waking brains the significance of the noise. After two and a half months we had received another visit from our elusive four-footed thief and this time it was not our valiant cockerel or our two geriatric ducks who would pay the ultimate price.

In more than a decade of backyarding we had been very fortunate in our losses: never before the previous harsh winter had a predator killed our poultry. Though the garden is bounded by a field the proximity of the goat shed to the chicken house has probably been responsible for our security. At the first hint of an intruder the goats are out to investigate, scaring off potential thieves.

This particular December the constant rain had turned the run into a quagmire, each evening as the light faded I would feed the livestock, then secure the door of the goat shed to keep the goats out of the mud and protect their dry bedding.

John had just finished a week of nights so hadn't surfaced at all in daylight. I had been doing the animal chores at both ends of the day. When there are twenty or so hens, all much alike, it is easy not to notice a couple are missing, especially when it never stops raining and your mind is on the warmth of the house and comfort. Besides I had understood that foxes killed indiscriminately and would have expected to come across a scene of mass destruction if we had been visited by one.

By the time John came off night shift and began asking questions we were down to fourteen hens, our cockerel had disappeared and the only sign of our two ancient Khaki Campbell ducks was a feather and some innards found after a search of the field behind us. The next morning we had thirteen hens, then twelve – the culprit was using us like a supermarket. Whatever our aversion to traps we had no option if we wanted to have any poultry left.

Each morning we would race to the window to see if anything was caught in the wire the local gamekeeper had fixed for us. The disappearances ceased and life settled back to normality. Weeks dragged into months, snow blanketed the earth and all was quiet. Other people lost ducks far more dramatically than us, then the night raids stopped as suddenly as they had begun.

The vixen came with the dawn: she crept under the fence exactly as before, this time the snare was waiting, the wire caught around her middle and held fast.

Enter Vic, our cowman neighbour: he spotted the fox, unaware she was unable to get away and, not able to rouse us, he raced home for his twelve bore shotgun and blasted off from half-way across the garden.

I was relieved not to have to deal with a live animal, though the gamekeeper was liable to be less pleased that the fox's pelt had been so damaged. Looking at the beautiful vixen, the first I had ever seen, it was impossible not to regret the need to snare such an attractive animal, but the alternative was a death sentence for our remaining chickens: sentiment versus reality.

In discussing fox's reputations for mass slaughter, a countryman observed that when the fox enters an enclosed space, the fowls not unnaturally panic, and that is what seals their fate. As long as they flutter and squawk the fox will perceive a threat and react by attacking everything that moves. If they remain still, the animal will only kill what it needs.

🦃

Ducks can be kept where there is no running water, but they are messy to have around. The first thing they do on spying a bucket of clean water if to delve into the feed or the earth, then straight to the bucket, swish about, then out with enthusiasm to make mud puddles. The goats, notoriously finicky, won't touch the dirty water and, as they share a run, this causes problems.

Our ducks were always Khaki Campbells, very good laying birds. The eggs were either sold to gourmets to whom a duck egg is a gastronomic treat, or cooked at home. They should never be used raw or soft boiled but otherwise are perfectly acceptable at the table.

We had been given our first duck eggs hatched by Doris, a very broody bantam. She was a tiny, fussy little hen with a crown of feathers on her head. On her arrival in the chicken run she had barely survived an attack by the other hens which left her limp and bleeding. John had rescued her and nursed her and for a while she conceived a violent passion for him. Whenever he appeared out of the back door she would follow him, clucking at his heels, embarrassingly devoted. She was the epitome of besotted motherhood, regardless that her brood rapidly became much bigger than herself and had such peculiar habits.

We had two ducks and a very handsome drake we called Fancy Pants: he strutted proudly and was master of all he surveyed.

His downfall was a fluffy white silkie bantam with blue face and legs, Pouffe by name. Ignoring his contemporaries, Fancy Pants would pursue Pouffe around the run, up and under the hen house with rape on his mind. At first we watched his amorous antics with amusement, but once he cornered the object of his desire the feathers flew. For the sake of our white puffball to whom I was much attached, Fancy Pants was given away.

When our next batch of eggs produced two drakes we were uncertain what to do with them. We had in the past taken unwanted cockerels to market but our hens stay with us until they die of old age. I prefer to cook anonymous frozen chickens from the supermarket than our worn-out hens.

¶

We did pass some cockerels to George Bennett who lives in a nearby hamlet so that he could fatten them for the pot. George is a real village character with his rosy cheeks, local accent and woolly hat. He is also one of life's victims – if anything is going to happen to anyone it will happen to George. He is a natural clown, sad and funny at the same time.

Only George riding home from work on his moped would be almost decapitated by a telephone wire as it blew across the road. Only George would then be rescued by the local Member of Parliament, less than happy at the fact our hero is bleeding copiously over his shiny, bright limousine. John happened to be passing in the police van, and trundled the poor little man off to hospital with dispatch.

George lovingly tended the young birds, fattened them and reported on their progress with pride. When the time came to wring their necks, he plucked them and hung them, only to have them disappear down the throat of a canine thief. It could only happen to George: he bewailed his misfortune, the rest of us commiserated with him and hid our smiles.

But, to return to the drakes: we could have kept one but I didn't relish choosing one for the pot. Few males are needed in nature, but I would prefer to make other arrangements than send the surplus to slaughter.

Inspired by the film 'Born Free', I suggested we find a lonely stretch of river and release the drakes into the wild. We put the drakes in a sack and drove to a remote spot. Donning our Wellingtons we each took a bird, waded into the stream and released them. After the initial panic-stricken flapping, the back garden reared drakes suddenly discovered the joy of their new habitat: they splashed and dived, obviously fascinated by the novel environment they found themselves in.

Our next fowl experience came when we were talked into housing a pair of pet geese when their owner had to move. 'They will be no trouble,' we were assured, an understatement of gigantic proportions. We couldn't let them loose in the garden, so they had to coexist with the chickens and the goats. They chased the former and attacked the latter, two of whom were in a delicate condition, with kids due any day. We needed to get rid of the geese immediately.

We found a field near the river a few miles away; Mr. Jackson, who allowed us to graze our lambs on his paddock, was prepared to house the geese temporarily. I rang the owners and explained new quarters had been found, and could they remove their pets from our vicinity.

The owner arrived with his son in a very old, bone-shaking van, the idea being that, while he drove, the boy and I would each hold a goose on our lap for the journey. The days when I was terrified of chickens pecking my ankles might have gone but to this day I have an aversion to handling birds with their beaks and claws and feathers. Besides, very large birds at close quarters make me nervous. I could hardly admit this to strangers, so I wrapped a sack around my goose's wings as tight as I dared, gritted my teeth and got into the van.

Until that moment I had thought my most uncomfortable ride was when we brought three nervous piglets home in the car, and discovered that when they are upset their bowel movements are frequent and particularly unpleasant. The proximity of the wicked beak that hovered within inches of my eyes convinced me I would be pecked in the face, unless the powerful wings were freed first, in which case I would more than likely have a broken neck, contrived to make this a ride I would never wish to repeat. When we eventually disembarked, still tightly clutching our feathered burdens, my gander, sensing freedom, struggled out of my arms and into the undergrowth, never to be seen again.

Goats Galore

L ulu had been a pet nanny who had never been mated. When her owner moved on she left the goat with an elderly lady who had a large paddock adjoining her house. The lady fed and cared for her charge but had neither the strength nor the knowledge for the tasks that needed to be done. After a while the results of this unintentional neglect became evident.

Lulu's udder, which filled with fluid as she grazed, was never milked out: her teats grew enlarged, one of them so badly that both my hands together could not encircle it. The udder poked monstrously between the goat's back legs which made her walk with a peculiar, skipping gait.

One morning a villager knocked at the door and asked if I could take a look at Lulu – he had seen her in the paddock and was convinced that all was not well.

The goat was a brown and white Toggenburg, she was frisking in the field when we arrived, seemingly content. On closer inspection it was obvious she needed immediate attention. Her feet were badly overgrown, the effect was rather like ingrowing toenails, Lulu could only hobble. John got out his sheath knife and began to cut. Lulu was not impressed, she was even less happy when I tried to milk her. It was reminiscent of the steer-wrestling seen at rodeos. Lulu wriggled and fought, we had no place to attach her so John held her collar while I grasped her udder. Lulu swivelled her rear end, knocking me flat on my back and upsetting John face downwards in the dirt, all three of us in an ungracious heap. Despite all our efforts not a drop of fluid could I coax out of the udder and the vet was called to drain the teat.

It was vital that the goat be milked regularly or the problem would recur, travelling to milk was a temporary measure. The lady asked if we would give Lulu a home; we were back to two goats after Holly's demise so we agreed to take her, intending to get her into condition, then pass her on.

However, we soon realized that no experienced goatkeeper would want such a useless animal; the udder was so distorted that if Lulu were ever got in kid the babies would never be able to suckle, and the thought of dealing with that teat, bulging with milk after kidding, was horrendous. With regular care the udder looked like a wrung-out dishcloth between Lulu's legs, but at least she could now walk properly. It took her a while to forgive us for the indignities we had heaped on her at our introduction, but she settled in and lived out the rest of her days in comfort.

White Billy was referred to us by another police station, after a desperate couple went seeking advice. They had been tempted by a cute baby animal and taken the kid as a pet, discovering to their cost the price of sentimentality. An unscrupulous goatkeeper had sold them a kid he said was weaned and would be useful keeping the grass down, besides being an ideal playmate for their small son.

The couple had struggled with the kid for a month, bought a shed and fencing, only to find that the animal had no intention of remaining where he was intended to be. With no companion, the human family became his herd and he would clear any obstacle to be with them.

When he arrived with us he was only as big as my month-old kids. It was likely he had been a week old when he had been handed over. He needed regular milk for up to four months, yet had been surviving on only a pint of pasteurized milk a day. He was too young to do more than mouth grass, and as goats are browsers not grazers he would never have doubled as a lawn mower. Added to this he had two very straight, sharp horns, likely to be lethal in close proximity to a small child.

We had three kids of our own at the time, and were prepared to raise White Billy with them on the understanding that when the time came he would go for meat with the other billies. There would be no cop-outs, sending him to market or finding him a home. Only well-bred male goats are used for breeding and, with multiple births in goats, billy kids are abundant. It is totally impractical to keep a male goat without a lot of space and, while they are adorable when they are tiny, they grow large, strong and seasonally smelly and can become a nuisance unless the owner is well aware of the pitfalls. Even the more productive and easier nannies have been ill-treated, intentionally or not, by people who never went into the practicalities of goatkeeping before buying a goat.

One such instance was added to John's case-load after a report to the RSPCA resulted in the Inspector, who admitted having no knowledge of goats, hedged his bets by quoting border line case, then walked away. The nanny had been bought as a lawn-mower, the owners had neither contacted local goatkeepers for advice nor read up on the subject. They later commented that they didn't know they had to feed her, they thought goats lived off the land. They will if they have a large enough area to roam unrestricted and access to shelter and a plentiful supply of herbage, but this animal was left tied on a domestic lawn in bitter winter weather. She had a few scraps thrown to her and a bucket of water; her only shelter was a hedge under which she cowered in the icy wind.

Goats should not be constantly tethered unsupervised; without a swivel on their chain they are inclined to tangle themselves up. In fact, this little nanny was found on several occasions wound around the stake so tightly she was unable to move. Goats also hate extremes of weather, excessive heat or cold or rain and someone should always be nearby to move them if conditions worsen. They are also pernickety eaters and will not even eat hay that has fallen from the manger and been trampled on, let alone short winter grass they have fouled.

No one can be expected to have a complete knowledge of all aspects of animal welfare. Due to being kept in such cold conditions the goat had grown a fluffy coat which made it look cute and plump, but underneath it was a bag of bones. The RSPCA Inspector refused to take the goat away, despite pleas from a local goatkeeper who was desperately trying to save the animal. Eventually and as a last resort she arrived at our door to make an official complaint.

It was already too late, by the time the warning was given and the time elapsed for it to be put into effect the goat was dead. A post mortem was carried out; malnutrition was diagnosed and the owners successfully prosecuted.

The next time there was a case of neglect it was reported straight to the police to sort out. In this case there was a happy ending – the goat was taken away and now lives a life filled with love and affection. The young woman who fought so hard to prevent suffering set up a goat rescue service, Rainbow Rescue, which is specifically a sanctuary for neglected and unwanted goats. The name comes from an old American Indian prophecy, 'When the earth is sick and the animals disappear the warriors of the Rainbow will come to protect the wildlife and heal the earth.'

Caroline Cannon was working locally when she began to take in strays of all descriptions – unwanted goats and dogs to begin with. When she lost the use of the land she housed the animals on she moved to Glebe land in Wyford, earmarked for future development, as a temporary measure. Caroline began life as a squatter, living in a dilapidated old caravan, while erecting animal sheds to house her growing animal family.

In the course of the next few years thirty goats, eighteen dogs, four sheep, six cats and a miscellany of chickens were amassed on the waterless site. During the very hot weather she drove a six-mile round trip five times a day to get water for her livestock. She worked in a nearby transport café and all her funds went to buy animal feed, pay vets' bills and run her ageing car. Local people had funds raised for her but life was a continual struggle.

After three years the inevitable conclusion loomed as the site was needed and Caroline had to move on. Premises to take 58 animals were in short supply: she had no money and no prospects – her beloved animals' fate looked grim, but her attitude was, 'If God wants me to look after the animals He will have to provide because I can't worry about it now.'

Thanks to publicity help was forthcoming. A lady in Surrey offered to buy some land to assure the animals' survival when she heard of the threatened eviction. Another couple bought and erected new sheds, while local builders provided materials. By the autumn the animal sanctuary was established. It was named Rainbow's End, proof that faith moves livestock as well as mountains!

Snoopy & Co.

John had been on a cycling holiday in Holland with his Venture Scouts. The nine days he was away had been uneventful; the weather had not been kind so lazy sunbathing was out of the question and an accident the fortnight before had put the goats' normal grazing field out of action until he was around to fix things. A lorry had skidded into the fence and through it, sending all three nannies in different directions. A neighbour had come to tell me there was a hole in the fence plugged only by a Hovis lorry. I raced down the road convinced that Snoopy, Tassy and Lulu would be exploring Wyford in varying directions or on their way home, sampling the forbidden delights of the gardens en route. Luckily they had not yet recovered from the fright of an extremely large vehicle coming at them and were in a huddle at the far end of the field.

Taking three goats is always a major undertaking when I am alone. I attach two dog leads to two collars, then thread one of the leads through the third goat's collar. With two goats on my right side and the other on my left I manoeuvre out of the gate and along the road feeling like Ben Hur bereft of his chariot.

In our garden we have a fenced-off area of rough ground where the goats can go for a change of scene from their run. Each dry day I had made use of this while John was away. Keeping the goats in the garden was a lot simpler than taking them to pasture, or so I thought – just move them from one run to another, easy!

On the day that John was due back I was returning the goats to the stable for the night. As always they were ready for their supper and pulling vigorously. The day I allowed my glamorous mother, in her tight skirt and high heels, to hold one of them homeward-bound, she was pulled off-balance the moment I let go of the lead and ended up with cut knees and shredded stockings, writhing in the road, while the errant animal made off without a backward glance. This evening I had a goat on each hand – Snoopy tugged and caught me unprepared, I let go and she was off to the vegetable plot. Knowing the impossibility of chasing one goat while leading another I swiftly returned Tassy to the run before cornering my runaway. Snoopy had been loose for seconds only, in passing she had grasped a mouthful of green potato apples, I was aware that they were not recommended feeding but had no idea how lethal they were.

The next morning Snoopy was abnormally difficult, slow and stubborn. As I led her out she went down on her knees, a not uncommon happening; goats have a nerve in their neck which if pinched will cause them to drop. Once the hold is loosened they get up and return to normal. Many a visitor wanting to take a goat for a walk has been horrified to see it apparently faint at their feet.

That evening Snoopy still appeared dozy. I determined if things were not right the next day I would call the vet, not connecting the goat's actions in any way with her brief spell of freedom.

The following morning it was obvious something was drastically wrong – Snoopy was unable to stand on her back legs. By now seriously alarmed, we called the vet who diagnosed some kind of poisoning. I knew she had not been out of the garden for two weeks so possible causes were limited, the only thing that made sense were the potato apples.

I more than half expected to be told my very first pet would have to be put down; the vet's only crumb of comfort was that she would either go downhill fast or get better slowly. He injected her, gave us some medicine and left.

For seventeen days Snoopy couldn't use her back legs. Everyday we got her to her feet – I supported her while John massaged her limbs to fight permanent paralysis and the danger of gangrene. Despite her disability she was perky and alert, ears pricked up and eating well. Our fears for her life subsided, slow recovery was obviously taking place.

Day eighteen dawned... this morning she was so ill, her balance was gone, she was moaning and uninterested in food. Before John went on duty she was obviously off-colour but as the morning progressed she became worse. I went to the goatshed and sat with her head in my lap, knowing the only kind thing to do was to end her pain.

I have seldom shed so many tears, she was eight-and-a-half years-old, the first pet either of us had ever had. All our married life she had been there – stubborn, disliking attention but part of the family. When John came home it was clear we couldn't allow her to suffer any longer. He borrowed a gun and shot her; it was an agonising thing to have to do.

Lulu meanwhile was showing signs of age; we decided we should find another goat to be a companion for Tassy, just in case. This was the only time we ever went looking for a goat; in the past and the future they have just turned up.

Ever since we began goat-keeping we have had black and white British Alpines, while both Lulu and Holly were Toggenburgs, light brown and white. The Sanaan breed is white, good milkers but I always think anaemic-looking and never wanted one. The Golden Guernsey is a lovely honey-gold colour but at this time rare in Britain which would make breeding complicated as mates would be few and far between.

The fifth breed is the Nubian or Anglo-Nubian. They have a variety of colours and markings and are distinguished by their Roman noses and their floppy ears. Unlike the other breeds which come into season from autumn to spring, the Nubians come into season every three weeks throughout the year.

Ever since attending my first Frome Cheese Show where there is a large goat section I have coveted one of these aristocratic animals. If I was going to choose a goat then I wanted an Anglo-Nubian. We found a person with three for sale and set off with high hopes.

We entered a dim stable where there were some of the biggest goats I had ever seen; they looked like small donkeys and had improbable names – Rose Red, Namesake and Twilight. The latter was the one we chose, with the proviso that if she didn't settle down she could be returned. Twilight was five years-old, had never kidded, had snowstorm mottled ears, a brown body and an impressive lineage.

The first thing she did on being led from her pen was to break away and leap the gate back to her stablemates. Once in our goatshed she cleared the walls of her stall and ended up atop the hay bales, much to her distress. John set to work raising the sides of the stall and I set to work wooing our latest pet. To begin with she was terrified of Lulu and Tassy, trying to hide behind me when they came to investigate this new creature, the like of which they had never seen before; I don't think they understood she was a goat at all.

Having changed homes, owners and companions it seemed unnecessarily cruel to alter her name as well, though to stand in the early evening dusk and shout 'Twilight' at the top of my voice made me feel pretty silly. So Twilly she became; John often referred to her as Dumbo, only partly because of her ears. It was true that she did seem less bright than the others. She had no notion of reverse – if instead of walking through a gate she walked behind it she stopped, totally confused. She would eat from a bowl, but apart from bread refused all hand-held titbits, and turned her nose up at sugar lumps which the others adored. Immensely strong, with no aggression in her make-up, timid to begin with, Tassy became her greatest friend. I never mated Twilly, and remained besotted with her until she died. All the little ones loved her, she was so gentle and allowed tiny fingers to pat her ears with tolerant patience.

❧

During our years of backyarding we have been lucky that vets have seldom been needed, though one problem that has recurred has been torn udders. This often happens in the spring when, after the winter confinement, the goats go into the lush, fresh pastures, the udders bulge with milk and barbed wire fencing is somewhere in the offing. To get to forbidden ground the goat pushes through obstacles, seemingly oblivious to the damage inflicted.

At her kidding before last Tassy produced one billy kid on a Friday, henceforth that became his name. The very first day of being parted from her kid Tassy cut her udder severely, severing the milk duct on one side. Although it didn't seem to bother her, the sight of the empty quarter on the wounded side, not to mention the blood-drenched leg, certainly bothered me.

The vet came, doped and stitched Tassy up with the help of my unflappable husband at the business end, while I held her head, murmuring endearments, more for my sake than hers. The patient was left propped against straw bales with me playing nurse until the anaesthetic wore off and she could stand unaided and return to the goatshed.

The immediate problem was getting milk from the newly stitched udder in the days ahead. With great reluctance Friday had to live apart from his mother to prevent unsupervised suckling. Each day the pair were reunited and Friday's eager little mouth held to the uninjured teat. Then I would gently and gingerly ease the milk from the bag into the teat with my left hand and squeeze it out with my right. A tedious business which continued for two weeks while Tassy was kept off grass and on low rations to slow down milk production.

By now, tending goats is as natural as keeping house – a daily job. Each goat has a personality all its own, as individual as people. They are crotchety, loving, irritating, determined, bossy or playful; comedy and tragedy intertwined. Only in her dying did Snoopy ever give us anything but pleasure. Everything began with her, that it continues to this day must be her legacy to the future.

Moving Moments

Ronald (whom we first met in chapter 3) and his mother lived in a house which was totally unsuitable for habitation; over the years it had become more and more dilapidated, there was no electricity and from the outside it looked derelict. It was more than a mile from the nearest village, at the top of a steep hill. With her bad leg and no transportation Ronald's mother was housebound.

At one time the house was owned by the Water Board. Latterly a farmer rented the land from the military and therein lay the problem – eviction from Crown property is almost impossible, so though everyone concerned agreed the house should be condemned, unless the occupants left of their own accord they could not be forced into better accommodation. It wasn't that they were unwilling, but making the break seemed more than the old lady could accomplish, and she resisted all attempts to help.

When I first met Ronald's mother we conversed through the window. I heard the sorry tale of the need to be rehoused, the willingness to go anywhere, how no one cared! There were council houses but such occupants were liable to be an embarrassment wherever they were placed and suitable options were few and far between. In my innocence I decided to see what I could do. I rang the Chairman of the Housing Committee, got her out of the bath; the County councillor, got him in from the garden; and wrote a plaintive plea to our MP. Within a few weeks a house was on offer – no more isolation from the community, meals on wheels and a home help if necessary and comfort beyond anything they had experienced in the latter years at least.

I called to tell them the key was available for them to view. Mother opened the window. " Would you like to see the house tonight? We can collect you?"

"No thank you I wouldn't."

"Why not?"

"If I leave the house squatters will get in."

"Squatters?" Now she had lost me!

"They are on the Plain looking at the house through field glasses, this is just the kind of house they are looking for."

"There aren't any squatters, I live in the Police Station so I'd know if there were any."

"You don't live in the wilds like I do." Undeniably true!

"Well I will stay in the house and look after it while John takes you to see your new place."

"No, if you don't mind."

And there we stuck. John tried three times, first with the District Councillor and the key, then with the social workers, in both instances mother quoted the farmer as wanting her to be responsible and not leave the house. The next stop was confrontation with the farmer and a Ministry of Defence spokesman. She listened, she agreed she wanted to leave, demanded something in writing and still refused to budge. "I'm not moving to Wyford, people die there. That was unanswerable and we were back to square one.

Uninformed onlookers would be forgiven for thinking nobody cared; but behind the scenes social workers, housing officers, the local policeman, doctor and district nurse were all involved in trying to find an acceptable solution.

Ronald wanted so badly to move, his wider experiences in the world, attending an adult training centre where there was warmth and light had shown him another way of life. He spent whole mornings in the shower delighting in the feeling of being really clean. Back at home the deterioration was frightening: in the cold weather their only source of water was what the local garage delivered, the pipes froze and an inspection showed more water coming from them than from the taps. More cracks appeared in the structure and ceilings began to bulge.

Mrs. W. agreed in the coming months to accept two more houses, only to change her mind. I was convinced that she had become agoraphobic with the years of enforced confinement and would never leave the house on the hill.

At last another house became available, ideally situated, in a community that was small, with open fields behind and in front, a large garden and three bedrooms.

As a last resort it was decided that if the old lady agreed to the move the key would be presented one day and the removal done the next with no time for prevarication. The drawback was that if Mrs. W. refused the move, nothing could be done. She insisted she organise the move herself so a standby removal van was out of the question but, just in case, the military provided a lorry and the Council two men.

At ten o'clock on the appointed day John and I, dressed in very old clothes, rendezvoused at the house with two social workers, the housing officer and a Crown Agent with an assistant. John and Gwen went to the window. Mother wouldn't let anyone in, she was waiting for Mr. Blades to move her she told them. As Mr. Blades was in the cattle transportation business and lived locally John and the Crown Agent returned to Wyford where they found the lorry just about to set out for market. Mr. Blades had indeed received a garbled message about going to see Mrs. W. but had no idea what he was supposed to do, nor had he been told a time or a date. He agreed to divert so as to tell his would be customer he was only licensed to carry livestock. She seemed satisfied and allowed us to enter the house.

Any thoughts of a speedy removal being accomplished were soon dashed – no furniture was to leave the house until the outside things were on the lorry. She then opened a cubby hole where coal, garden tools, wood, wire and chimney brushes all jostled for space. I received my first inclination that my husband's airy assumption that things were old but clean had been far off the mark and the men on the lorry, supposedly there to help, refused point blank to come into the house. They were concerned about vermin and although they would put things on the lorry the fetching and carrying was for the rest of us. The other two women were respectably dressed, Gwen having an appointment at lunch time which meant she had to leave after a couple of hours.

Now the fun began in earnest: after one lorry-load Gwen managed to convince Mrs. W. that the contents of all the outhouses would not fit into her new abode. John told the old lady firmly that if some of the sacks were rubbish she must leave them for the dustmen. She accepted this readily – I had been trying to be gently tactful and getting nowhere.

Her furniture was old and cumbersome: at some time it had been valuable but twenty years in the house had taken its toll. No one before had been allowed all over the house so the amount to be transported came as an unwelcome surprise. Whatever its condition everything had to go. We were all so relieved that the move was taking place no one dared upset the delicate balance of negotiations.

Gwen explained she had to leave; would Mrs. W. let PC Wyeth take her to her new house? The little lady, who reached little further than my husband's waist glared up at him fiercely. "Can I trust you" she demanded.

Gwen tried reasoning, "You know PC Wyeth, he's a policeman, of course you can trust him."

"No, you can't trust all policemen you know," and out came an old story that only John could unravel.

At some time in the distant past a police driving school car with four officers on a driving course had seen Ronald making his erratic progress on his moped and stopped to check him out. To Mrs. W. four huge policemen pouncing on her son had made an indelible impression. "Are you going to take me to Bristol?" she asked. John assured her he was only taking her to the new house four miles away. Mrs. W. nodded sagely, then continued to oversee her possessions being transferred to the lorry.

Fortunately the journey to the new house was short but it was evident that the do-it-yourself move needed more hands. The Housing Officer and the Crown Agent set about getting more lorries after lunch.

' I went with the lorries to the new house while John remained at the old. Getting the final lot of furniture down the rickety stairs he decided that, as the house was set for demolition, if they pulled the bannister out they would have more room. In the event the bottom stairs went too, leaving Ronald upstairs and having to be rescued, an exciting postscript to his day.

Five trips had to be made and the house filled up at an alarming rate. The housing officer, Gloria, and I attempted to make the house look more home-like, moving furniture so that the place appeared less like a warehouse and more lived in. The men sweated over large wardrobes and huge cupboards, and a dilapidated three piece suite included a mouse which disappeared into the chaos.

At long last Mrs. W. and Ronald came into sight, both seemingly impressed with what they saw. We had tried to place things where they were likely to be needed. John took out his spanner and began putting the awkward metal bed frames back together. We had put Mrs. W. in the largest bedroom. Ronald chose his room and identified his bed and dressing table, "the smart one". Compared to the others it was too.

Mrs. W came into the room – no, she didn't want the best bedroom, she wanted the other one, the smallest room where we had piled the suitcases, boxes of clothes, spare drawers and a couple of chests. Earmarked as the box room, the 'matchbox room' as Ronald dubbed it on sight, it was presently cluttered with the debris of twenty years, but the larger, airier room held no attraction for the incorrigible old lady.

The bed, just painstakingly put together, would not fit through the doors. So out came the spanner, down came the frame, along the hall and up again amid the confusion of possessions.

Outside there were several pieces of furniture that wouldn't fit in. Mrs. W. wanted the huge brown wardrobe brought into the house – protests that there was no room for it were dealt with summarily. It could go in the bathroom which was on the ground floor at the side of the house. It was blatantly obvious the only way it would fit in was in front of the toilet, blocking the doorway. Mrs. W. didn't mind, she had already stored her carpet in the bath tub so the wardrobe's incongruity fitted right in with the Alice in Wonderland feel of the whole day. Then Bob had a

brainwave: the wardrobe would just fit behind the back door as long as it didn't have to open too wide. Mrs. W. was quite happy with this compromise.

Before we left we went to the local shops and bought bread, cheese, ham and milk and promised to return the next day. We left two pieces of furniture in the garden, the shed with enough room for Ronald's moped and the pair having been shown how to turn on the stove and where the light switches were.

❦

It had taken seven hours and five trips to get the job done; the atmosphere at the end was holiday-like. One of the men who had been helping on the lorry since the beginning confided in me that when he first saw me he thought I was one of them there hippies until he saw what was needed and realized I was dressed for the job in hand. I admit I laughed, but recalling the dilapidated building he had seen me coming out of I took a look at my ancient anorak, used for animal-tending over the years so pretty scruffy. It went in the dustbin that very night. Remembering the tourists who have stopped to take my photograph when they have seen me walking the goats home from pasture I imagined them going to their distant homelands with a picture of what they fondly imagine is an English peasant. My work clothes made me look like Compo in 'Last of the Summer Wine' – a new image was definitely called for!

The following day we arrived hot on the heels of the doctor who was checking that the move had not been too traumatic an experience for its participants. It was the rest of us who were traumatised: the W.'s seemed to have thrived on the excitement! They were both in fine fettle having been up since dawn moving things. The shed was filled to overflowing with no sign of Ronald's moped. An old white cupboard that in the old house had stored the food had been pushed in front of the walk-in larder and a two ring gas burner was in pride of place while the new electric cooker stood ignored in the corner.

"Ah," said Mrs. W, "will you move a cupboard from the garden into the other room."

"There is no room," quoth I, remembering the clutter of the day before.

"Oh yes there is." Triumphantly the old lady led the way. All the furniture was stacked against the wall at one end of the room, while Ronald's moped stood under the window. She was right, they did have plenty of space. "And I want the council to take away the settee and chairs!" Yesterday she had insisted that they moved, today they were redundant. I imagined the faces of the men who had struggled and sweated the day before, returning to dispose of the suite.

John and the doctor between them staggered into the house with the required furniture and placed it where they were directed. Now a perfectly happy Mrs. W. wanted to know where she could purchase one of the Army huts she could see from her window. John disillusioned her by saying they were old-fashioned and not made any more, but suggested she ask the council for a lean-to instead.

We left the pair perfectly content with their lot having recreated as nearly as possible the environment they had just left. They were now within a community, one of their neighbours helped put up the required shed and dug their garden and they were still on John's patch so he could keep an eye on them. After three years the story had a happy ending!

Animal Antics

In all the articles and books you see on self-sufficiency the sun is always shining, there is no mud and everywhere looks immaculate, totally unlike real life! But during one scorching summer we had a wonderfully hot spell when barbecues were possible, shorts were the order of the day (even if in my case they were worn with Wellington boots) and the earth baked instead of squelched.

At the end of April we bought three little pigs, seven weeks-old and ready to face the great outdoors. Our animal pens form three sides of a square with a vegetable plot in the middle. This particular year John decided to fence it off as a temporary pig playpen. There were stumps from the winter greens, root vegetables that had been overlooked, nettles and clumps of grass in profusion.

At first the piglets were all very timid. Each time we approached they would snuffle, jump and with one accord hide in the furthest corner of the sty, emerging gingerly, snouts aquiver to make sure we had gone. When they discovered the gate to the sty opened into a new world they were initially wary of the unexpected freedom and all the inviting things to chew.

John's idea was that the pigs would turn the earth and then he would plant it. However, we managed with the three other vegetable plots that year, so all summer long the piglets rooted and dug to their hearts' content. To our surprise they ate nettles with every indication of enjoyment and, once they overcame their first suspicion of us, we would go into the garden and turn the earth for them.

We did worry they might get heatstroke and become roast pork on the trotter, so we gave them hose showers now and then, which they adored. Their pleasure seemed quite sensual as they squirmed and wriggled and fought each other off, occasionally standing, mouths agape for a cold drink.

As they grew they became more adventurous. One morning there was no sign of them, in the pen or the sty. Visions of prowling pink porkers almost in their prime began to form. Then I noticed the stable door hanging drunkenly on its hinges. Investigation showed the piglets had dug under the fence into the goat run, causing minor chaos with hysterical fowls and disapproving goats. In fact they escaped twice more in the same way, then began looking over the tin fence which had held them captive so well in the past and now tilted alarmingly. It was back to the sty after that.

A job we really looked forward to each year was helping out at a friend's farm at sheep-dipping time. The tradition began when we had to take our pet lambs to be dipped, an experience very new to us. The trouble with hand-reared lambs is that they have no notion of being driven: they insist on following, very much Rosemary's little lambs. Leading them into the sheep dipping trough is not to be recommended, so fun and games was had by all, manhandling being necessary. It is often needed with the flock too, the older ewes know what is coming and have no desire for the dip. They are fat and stubborn and often need brute force to make them enter the water.

Dipping is essential to get rid of the dreaded fly. In hot weather flies land on the sheep and lay their eggs in any warm, moist place they find, frequently under the tail where the animal may be messy. In the fullness of time the eggs hatch into maggots, which bury themselves through the fleece and begin to feed on the living body of the sheep. It is very painful for the sheep and bleeding patches can be seen through the wool. In extreme cases this can cause death.

Our second pair of lambs, Starsky and Hutch, were found to have maggots and a very uncomfortable time we all had. We filled a tin bath with Jeyes Fluid and immersed the lambs' rear ends in it. As they were lifted from the home-made dip maggots fell dying on the ground around them, a sight guaranteed to put you off your dinner.

Watching the flock come off the hills is a stirring sight to town-bred eyes. Sheep are herd animals and a flock moves as one body if properly handled – it's amazing that one person and a dog can move so many animals.

My job was keeping the dipping pens filled so that the flow was unimpeded. Once they begin to run it's an easy job, they follow each other into the dip without hesitation, but after five or six have entered the water the run has to be halted so that the sheep in the dip have a full minute before being let into the pens to dry out. This means they have to be started again frequently, and manhandling is often the only way a fat ram with his heels dug in can be persuaded to get into the dip. After all these years John has become an expert at this, Paul the farmer would make sure the sheep's head goes under so the animal is completely immersed and his wife Rome separated the animals at the far end to dry off.

At my last dipping session I did a stint in the middle of the trough with a broom to push the sheep under, it was a very damp job! The men were wearing waterproof trousers. Paul was pushing sheep from the holding pen into the chute and John was getting them into the water. The first animals had to be coaxed or coerced in and I was able to stand clear but the last lot were young, inexperienced with dips and hand-reared so they bounced in enthusiastically, sending tidal waves over the side of the trough, making sure that this year at least my nether regions would repel all insects. My jeans were soaked, I had dip in my eyes and hair and only barely avoided a dunking myself as I almost overbalanced in my eagerness to make sure I baptised the animals sufficiently. It was me and my broom and John and his hefty foot that made sure the job was done.

On one occasion as I was holding the pen gate open a small lamb raced out, hitting me a glancing blow behind my knees. The gate was already swinging shut. Instinctively I held on, the gate moved on almost wrenching my shoulder from its socket and my rear end hit the ground with a thud, right in a patch of manure. Rome, despite the twinkle in her eye, rushed to see if I was alright while my unchivalrous husband doubled over with merriment.

❦

For Wiltshire officers June is a time of being constantly available. The longest day on the 21st June has been a focus as the new age travellers' convoys converge on the prehistoric monument of Stonehenge on Salisbury Plain for the Summer Solstice. This unwelcome yearly invasion has been going on a great many more years than the media focus might lead one to suppose.

In years when sections of the convoy move through the Wylye Valley farmers block off every road and track and in some instances stand guard to prevent mass trespass. No doubt if small groups wished to bed down overnight and would leave as promised the next day then few would object. The problem is sheer weight of numbers, intimidating in itself. The cries for human rights are very one-sided: for far too long the rights of the people who live and work in Wiltshire were ignored.

John is very even-tempered, the only time he ever lost his sense of humour completely with the animals was after a particularly trying night shift. The month before had been very dry and he had raised his plants carefully in the greenhouse, planted them out, watered them lovingly and each night had squashed the teeming aphids with his fingers.

John had been up all night over the solstice and was on a quick change-over shift to go to work at 4pm. I had been out to lunch with three friends and we had all come back to the house for home-made lemonade.

I had left the goats in the side enclosure so, when Nora called she could see a goat in the garden, I remarked she should be able to see three and carried on with the refreshments. She didn't think to mention the goat in question was under the window eating the flowers! John, just surfacing from the depths of sleep, looked out to see the goat happily munching his precious plants while underneath him we gossiped and giggled. Tassy had demolished more than a hundred lovingly tended plants in minutes, and was having a wonderful romp; John saw all his efforts disappear down a rapacious throat.

I ran into the garden to try and catch the four-legged vandal, but a straight skirt and high heels are not recommended wear for chasing goats. Tassy raced past me, I grabbed at her collar, was swung round and fell flat on my back while she skipped on to pastures and plants new. The other three women were little help, all of us hampered first by our clothing and then by our mirth. My husband was stern-faced and very cross; he viewed me spreadeagled on the ground, winded and dusty and acidly remarked if I was going to fall down I might at least keep hold of the goat.

Afterword

Nothing lasts forever. The early years of adjustment and adventure, adapting to the rural lifestyle and carving our own niche within the community were exciting and rewarding.

Policing methods have changed enormously even in the twenty-four years since we moved into an empty house with a derelict garden, and fulfilled a role which was even then becoming part of the past. The story continues but now it has moved on. The days of poachers and poisoned owls, of animal escapades and country police stations are gone forever.

Romy Wyeth
October 1997

COUNTRY BOOKSHELF

from Ex Libris Press presents the following books:

MARCH WINDS & APRIL SHOWERS
Country Weather Lore by Ralph Whitlock
80 pages; Illustrated with Bewick engravings; Price £3.50

THE SECRET LANE by Ralph Whitlock
A Country Story set in the 1930s.
152 pages; Price £4.95

LETTERS FROM THE ENGLISH COUNTRYSIDE
by Ralph Whitlock
Topics included here are firmly rooted in the traditional life of the countryside. A nostalgic but wry view of the past is balanced by an often humorous commentary on the present.
160 pages; Numerous pen & ink drawings; Price £4.95

CHRISTIANA AWDRY'S HOUSEHOLD BOOK
by Margaret Jensen
Recipes and cures selected from an eighteenth century household book.
128 pages; Pen & ink drawings; Price £4.95

GRAN'S OLD-FASHIONED REMEDIES, WRINKLES AND RECIPES
by Jean Penny
Remedies for common ailments; wrinkles, or tips, to save time and effort about the house; recipes using inexpensive ingredients to create mouth-watering dishes: all are included within these pages.
96 pages; Numerous engravings; Price £3.50

GRAN'S OLD-FASHIONED GARDENING GEMS by Jean Penny
Packed full of tips and details aimed at the reluctant gardener for whom the 'garden in bloom' is more often 'that blooming garden.'
96 pages; Numerous engravings; Price £3.50

MY NEW FOREST HOME by Irene Soper
This account reflects a spirit of tranquillity and timelessness embodied by the Forest itself and is a lasting testament of one who knows and loves this memorable mandscape.
128 pages; Illustrated; Price £4.95

THE ROMANY WAY by Irene Soper
At times anecdotal, at times factual, but always sympathetic and informative, this book is a joyous but gentle celebration of a unique people.
112 pages; Fully illustrated ; Price £4.95

LAND GIRL by Anne Hall
Her story of six years in the Women's Land Army, 1940-46
One woman's recollection of six years dedicated to the Women's Land Army. The many photographs and the author's text combine to produce an honest, evocative and personal portrayal of a unique chapter in our social history.
144 pages; Illustrated throughout; Price £4.95

LUMBER JILL by Mavis Williams
Her story of four years in the Women's Timber Corps, 1942-45
A personal account of a time when women used primitive methods to cut down trees to make pit-props for the coal mines and fuel to produce charcoal.
96 pages; Illustrated; Price £3.95

VILLAGE PRACTICE by Anne Stratford
A Year in the life of a Country Doctor's Wife
A story told with fondness and a gentle humour – a heartwarming read.
160 pages; Illustrated; Price £4.95

GROWING WITH THE GRAIN by Richard Mack
A Farming Story
A rich and rewarding account of a farm apprenticeship in 1961.
160 pages; Illustrated; Price £4.95

WINIFRED by Sylvia Marlow
Her childhood and early working life
Winifred Spencer was born in 1899, the daughter of a cowman and his wife and one of thirteen children. Unsentimental and honest, this is Winifred's story of her struggle to survive.
128 pages; Illustrated throughout; Price £4.50

MAISIE & ME by Stella Ashton
A Country Childhood in the 1920s
The sights, sounds and smells of the countryside come alive in Stella Ashton's recollections of her childhood. Words and pictures combine to produce a loving portrait of a world past, but not forgotten.
80 pages; pen & ink drawings; Price £3.95

These books may be obtained through your local bookshop or direct from the publisher, post-free, at
1 The Shambles, Bradford on Avon, Wiltshire, BA15 1JS.

In addition to the above books, Ex Libris Press also publishes books on the West Country and the Channel Islands. Please ask for our free illustrated list.